D1614564

BANNERMAN

Lord Bannerman.

Photograph by George Russell, Paisley.

BANNERMAN

THE MEMOIRS OF
LORD BANNERMAN OF KILDONAN

Edited by

JOHN FOWLER

IMPULSE BOOKS

ABERDEEN 1972

First Published 1972 by
Impulse Publications Ltd.,
28 Guild Street,
Aberdeen,
Scotland.

1972

Printed by Gee and Son, Chapel Street, Denbigh.

CONTENTS

FOR RAY

If you met John Bannerman you felt the better for
it, even if you only had three words with him.
— HERBERT WADDELL.

PREFACE

WHEN Lord Bannerman died in May 1969 he left his memoirs unfinished. My task has been twofold : I have revised and edited the manuscript in detail and I have tried to fill in briefly the most obvious gaps in his incomplete narrative. The revision ranged from tidying careless wording to major surgery on what was still a loosely organised early draft.

John Bannerman — whether through ill health, lack of time or reticence — left some awkward blanks in his story. For example, he has little to say about family and home after childhood, although his family life was rich and warm, and nothing about his life peerage and brief parliamentary career. I have provided a little of what was missing in the form of linking passages based on material supplied in interviews with some of his friends and acquaintances. The list of such people could have been endless, but time was limited; besides, this is his book, not mine.

In particular I wish to thank his sister Morag Bannerman, James Crampsey, Lady Jean Fforde, Robert Hay, factor to Montrose Estates, Jack House, James Ireland, Russell Johnston, M.P., James J. MacGregor (who kept a valuable diary of the car trip across America), the Rev. Donald MacLeod, Hugh Macphee, David Steel, M.P., Herbert Waddell and the Bannerman family John, Calum, Janet and Elizabeth. Chrissie Bannerman and Lachlan MacKinnon gave valuable help with the manuscript, and I am also grateful to Jack Webster of the *Scottish Daily Express* for his advice. I think it is fair to say that without the initial interest shown by Ian McColl, now Editor of the *Daily Express,* this book would not have reached the public.

Above all, I must thank Ray, Lady Bannerman, for her faith and determination to see these memoirs in print. Without her encouragement it is doubtful whether the book would have been either written or published, and it is to her that John Bannerman would have dedicated his work if he had lived.

JOHN FOWLER.

FOREWORD

by The Rt. Hon. Jo Grimond, M.P.

I WAS once, for some good Liberal reason which now escapes me, having a drink in a charming Welsh hillside pub, when Johnny Bannerman arrived. He was about an hour late. He came out of sheer good-will, all the way from Scotland. His arrival gave great pleasure. He would always come, not always at the right time, nor indeed always to the right place, but his arrivals always gave pleasure. He liked his fellow men and they liked him. And that is why he has written such a good autobiography — so startlingly good in many respects. The early passages, in particular, about his life in Glasgow and visits to Tiree, about his father's friends and rugby football, are brilliant — and brilliantly short. I suppose I ought to have known that extrospection could produce a better autobiography than introspection, but I confess that when I was asked to write this preface I wondered how anyone as little interested in himself as Johnny seemed to be could write a biography at all. Here it is. And it retains some pictures which will be of enduring historical importance to anyone interested in the extraordinary world of the Gaels. One is of communion week in Applecross, another is a ceilidh and the last is the story of a light-as-a-feather toy and how he waded through a midden in pursuit of it. Any decent lowland Scot or indeed Orkney-man or Shetlander would have fished it out with a pole or rake — especially if by some ill chance they had been dressed in a kilt. Not so young Master Bannerman. I suppose it was a foretaste of the habits of someone who was arguably the best rugby forward of all time.

How anyone as gentle as Johnny could have played rugger so well remains a mystery. Though extrovert he was very far from being domineering or ambitious. Not only good manners but his natural desire that others should talk and shine made him indeed rather self-effacing. Perhaps this was his Celtic ancestry. The Celts seem to combine ferocity with a certain self-depreciation or modesty. Politically this mixture has served them ill. Johnny tells again and again how he resented the treatment of the Highlands by London

11

and the English landlords. And certainly I sympathise. But was the main responsibility that of the English? We suffered the unspeakable Cumberland and many unattractive speculators from the South. But do the clan chiefs themselves come out of the story very well? Or the Highland lawyers and factors? And what has always struck me is the docility with which the crofters accepted the Clearances. In many ways this was a tribute to their innate human qualities, but it has not been entirely beneficial to their land. Johnny speaks too of how he himself in his political campaigns suffered from the establishment. But why, with the ballot secret, did the electorate suffer the establishment? If he is right in alleging that a factor in his defeat at Inverness was the introduction of a Labour candidate whose declared aim was to attack Bannermanism and for whom this was the only appearance as a candidate in the constituency, is it not strange that the Highlanders should be influenced by such people and the stable from which they come? I admire Johnny for making no bones about his resentment. But I wonder if he was a natural politician? He says he was not thick-skinned. We must believe him, though he certainly was not embittered. He certainly had what is now called charisma. He had knowledge and talents and a sound grounding in economics. But he did not organise himself as a politician — more credit to him some people will say. In politics the heart must use the head and the heart must also sense the political moment as when in 1968-69 Scotland really might have had the independence she deserved. Scottish hearts and heads are not always in tune.

The Liberal Party owes him much. However, he at least ended up briefly as a Life Peer; which is more than the Party has been able to offer many stalwart Liberals of modern times. And he has left us these bits of autobiography — scraps they may be, but very digestible and well put together by the Editor, though I would not accept all Mr. Fowler's judgements. I have no doubt that Johnny asked the recording angel " I pray thee then write me as one who loves his fellow men " and as in the case of Ben Adhem I equally have no doubt that the Almighty rated him very highly.

J. GRIMOND.

1

BIAS—OR A POKE OF PEPPERMINTS

IF you can assure your audience that your speech will not be long they heave a sigh of relief and listen with some resignation for you to prove yourself a liar. That is why the most eagerly awaited phrase in a sermon is " finally and in conclusion ". Teeth grind the diminishing peppermint in thanksgiving.

With a book it is different. Nothing compels you to take it up and read. You thumb over its pages and you decide to read it or throw it away.

I need not declare this book to be short. You can see that for yourself. Nor has it any intellectual claim; that will be self-evident. In this book I give you the essence of my experience of living in Scotland since the first of September 1901, the date of my birth in the Shawlands district of Glasgow. It is not the vanity of a detailed account of my life, for were it merely an autobiography I think you would be justified in buying a poke of peppermints rather than the book. If you tarry awhile at a few milestones in my personal and family life it is because these are also corner stones in the formation of what is unashamedly a Scottish outlook.

I admit that it is a biassed book, a prejudiced book. Pride in one's background is the salt of life, the savour that makes life appetising. The Englishman's pride is reflected in the song *There'll Always be an England*. What Scot worthy of the name would oppose the sentiment of *Scots Wha Hae*? If you cannot stomach another man's prejudices then it might be wiser to buy that poke of peppermints, or perhaps liquorice allsorts. This book is not for you.

If you read on, you must take me biassed as I am.

2

FATHER AND SON

It will be fortunate for young John in this world if ever he gets fame higher than that he was the son of his father — the Rev. Donald Lamont of Blair Atholl.

He was an example of the true Gael at his best and noblest — the Rev. Calum MacLeod of Balquhidder.

(Excerpts from obituary notices on the death of John Roderick Bannerman in 1938.)

Returning home to the Strath of Kildonan with twelve grapeshot wounds in his body after the Battle of Waterloo, my great-grandfather reached Glasgow. He was told he need not go further. His people had been evicted from their croft along with the rest of the Bannermans of Kildonan and were now in Canada pioneering settlements on the Red River. Some helped to found the city of Winnipeg, where one of the oldest streets is named Bannerman Street.

Remaining in Glasgow, my great-grandfather shortly afterwards married a girl MacDonald from Ho-beag in South Uist who was on a visit to her uncle in Glasgow. A male child of the marriage was born posthumously, for my great-grandfather succumbed to his wounds within a year, and his widow and child returned to South Uist, where her people were cartwrights and millers. From that fatherless boy stemmed the only Bannerman family in the Outer Hebrides.

In 1873 a combined potato famine and drought drove the Bannerman family from South Uist to settle in Glasgow, and so they added to the Highland immigrants who were to make Glasgow the greatest Highland city in the world. Among them was my father, then a young child.

I remember my father as a short, stocky man, strong of chest and shoulders, with a patrician head, blue eyes with a glint of

Hebrid seas in them and a generous mouth topped by a little sandy moustache. He was only seven years of age when he arrived in Glasgow with his family from the Isle of Uist. Gaelic was his only language, and it was to be as much the language of his home in Glasgow as though he were still in the mill house in South Uist. At thirteen, after attending a one-master school in High Street, he became a telegraph boy in the G.P.O. at a wage of a few shillings a week. His mother, Mary MacDonald, a bardess in her own right from Sollas, North Uist, decided that the Post Office spelt security and that to put her son even on the lowest rung was no mean achievement. The Highlander, driven by insecurity to forsake a way of life dear to him, clutched at any opportunity that might give him a new sense of permanency to compensate for the community life from which he had been wrested.

The Highlander's greatest asset is his insatiable desire for education. My father was no exception and night school supplied the opportunity. In the Glasgow High School night classes he would regularly earn a hundred per cent in the examinations. Judging from his erudition in later years his pursuit of knowledge did not stop there but continued through most of his adult life. A great friend of the family and relative of my mother, Angus Robertson — a famous crofter son of Skye and Gaelic novelist — used to tell me how he had read Gibbon's "Decline and Fall of the Roman Empire" three times in his youth, and to listen to conversation between Angus and my father was to hear discussion of a quality that would have done credit to a couple of Oxford dons. Do not think that there was any pomposity or artificiality in this, for it had a delightful spontaneity about it — wit and imagination and the laughter of keen enjoyment. To sit at the feet of such men was in itself an education that I could never have found in books.

My father eventually became a senior superintendent in the Glasgow G.P.O., but was never wholly reconciled to the impersonal officialdom of the Post Office. I am told, and indeed saw for myself, that he was beloved by all ranks in the great sorting office where he was latterly in charge of hundreds of men. It was known that his promotion to still higher office was retarded by a forthright, honest outlook which the Postmaster of the time did not like. My father refused to compromise or curry favour.

He had two worlds to live in — Gaelic and English — which I inherited. His Glasgow world was one of bustle and competition, of long hours of work, and the friendship of his Lowland colleagues.

But it was in the Gaelic world of home and Highland friends that
he found most pleasure. He was a co-founder of *Ceilidh Nan
Gaidheal,* the Highlander's Ceilidh, in Glasgow about 1890. It met
and prospered in my younger days in *Talla nan Clachairean,* the
famous Gael Lodge of the Freemasons, at 100 West Regent Street,
where two or three hundred men, women and youngsters would
come every Saturday night to hear a lecture and perhaps take part
in the discussion. Many a budding minister essayed public speaking
there for the first time and received excellent guidance and example
from the " elder statesmen " whose facility of speech and native
intelligence made their contributions a delight to hear. No word
of English was allowed to be spoken, and the evening would finish
with traditional Gaelic singing from members of the audience.

Though battered a bit after a rugby match, I was expected to
turn up if at all possible to these ceilidhs. I sang my first solo
Gaelic songs there, often when I would rather have been elsewhere
with the boys after a game. I attended, since my father would have
been disappointed if I had not turned up. He knew the true values
in life, and to learn something about my heritage from song and
story is one of these values.

I remember vividly such Highlanders as the erudite Malcolm
MacLeod, called *Calum na Fiasaig* (Calum of the Beard), from the
island of Lewis, later to become head of the Govan School Board,
Neil MacLaine (in Gaelic *Niall-an-Taillear* or Neil the Taylor —
not that he was a tailor, but even in Glasgow he was still known
by his Tiree patronymic), Hector MacFadyen, the Rev. Hector
Cameron and his brothers Dr. John and Hugh, McGregor Whyte
the artist, Hector MacDougall, Glasgow policeman and Gaelic
scholar from the island of Coll, and Hugh Macphee of Ballachulish,
a young man giving promise of his zeal for the Gaelic language
which he later used to such splendid purpose in the BBC and
An Comunn. Then there was Snodgrass — an excellent Gaelic
speaker whose first name I never knew but remember for his
un-Highland name. Donald Currie was a stocky little man known
mainly as *Ach co dhiubh* (meaning " Well, anyway " or " so be it ")
because he punctuated all he had to say with this phrase. He said
it in such a peculiar dialect and so often, when he needed a breath
or time to think, heaving his shoulders as he inhaled a new breath
or exhaled the last of the old, that many like myself just waited
for his gusty sighing " *Ach co dhiubh* " and cared little for what he
said between. He was also sometimes known as New York from
his references to the time he stayed there.

The exiled Highlanders of *Ceilidh nan Gaidheal* were men of varied callings — skippers, ministers, doctors, teachers, joiners, plumbers, policemen, shoemakers, artists — but all had the common sheet anchor of their Gaelic heritage. But perhaps they were too exclusive in their allegiance to Gaelic, for, as I have said, not a syllable of English was allowed at *Ceilidh nan Gaidheal* and special care was taken to translate into Gaelic even the most alien ideas, phrases or names. There was bitter feeling when the rival bilingual High School Ceilidh was set up about the same time. Today the Gaelic Ceilidh is extinct and the High School Ceilidh flourishes. There can be no doubt that the Gaelic Ceilidh improved the Gaelic of the natives who attended, but it closed the door to the learner of the language. On the other hand, I would say that although the bilingual ceilidh continues, there is less spoken Gaelic to be heard there than when it first started. There must be a middle course in this English world which will allow Gaelic to survive and to develop, for throw English and Gaelic into the same pool and there is no doubt as to which will eventually drown. To live against the overwhelming prestige of English, Gaelic must be given at least equality with other languages in the curriculum of Scottish schools.

Gaelic was John Bannerman's first language, not English, even though he was born and brought up in Glasgow. He and his sister Morag picked up English from their playmates, but the language of their home was Gaelic.

The preaching of the word for me was the Gaelic word in St. Columba Church, St. Vincent Street. *Tigh mo Chridhe, Tigh mo ghraidh,* house of my heart, house of my love, is inscribed above its door. My father was an elder in it from my earliest recollection. We travelled by tramcar to church on a Sunday morning from Shawlands and later from Giffnock. I can reach it today as quickly by car from my home at Balmaha as I did then by tramcar from Giffnock, but today I do not have my father saying to me " *Eirich, a Sheonaidh,* Get up, Johnny, if you can play football all Saturday you can get up and come to church on Sunday ". At that time I played soccer on the Saturday morning and rugby in the afternoon, and Sunday morning was a harsh awakening. Stiff and often bruised, neither flesh nor the spirit was willing. But the result was always the same. Slowly, reluctantly at first and then with resignation and even some pleasure, I would find myself alongside my father on the tramcar hurtling our way to St. Vincent Street to attend Gaelic service at 11 a.m.

After church we would disdain the tramcar till we reached Nelson Street, walking along with the Paisley Road West Highlanders, members of the Saturday night ceilidh. Neil the Tailor was a great, broad, hearty, kindly bearded Highlander, a bard of no mean quality with a gentle, beautiful wife, one son, and a large family of daughters. The name Ann must have figured largely in his ancestry for his teacher daughters all had names ending in Ann and even the son was Lachainn. Lachainn and I often lagged behind to visit ice-cream shops en route for Nelson Street.

But if the elders walked, their discussion was by no means pedestrian. It covered the sermon for the first half-mile, but by the time they came to Jamaica Bridge they could easily have been crossing the old hump-backed bridge over the burn " at home ", for talk and anecdote were far removed from Clydeside, far from the grey cobbles of Glasgow to the sheen white sands of Tiree and the Hebrides and back into the days of Ossian.

St. Columba was a worldly church in the estimation of some, compared to, say, the Gaelic Free Presbyterian Church of St. Jude's. Nevertheless, St. Columba Church was the satisfying spiritual centre for succeeding generations of Highlanders no matter how scattered their homes were in Glasgow. A grandson of Neil the Tailor, Neil MacLaine Cameron, is today session clerk of St. Columba, demonstrating the continuing loyalty of Highlanders to their established mother church in Glasgow.

It was through membership of the St. Columba Church Gaelic choir that my father met and married my mother, Mary MacDonald, whose family of many sisters and brothers had come to Glasgow from Harrapool, Broadford, Isle of Skye, in the 'seventies. She was gentle, blue-eyed, with raven black hair framing a Celtic face with high cheek bones. She died of heart trouble when I was thirteen, a gentle Highland lady. My father took years to recover from the blank left in his life.

He worried that our meals might not be nourishing enough, especially for me as my rugby became more strenuous. For several years we had a little Irish maid who saw to the house but was no cook. She was cheerful and happy, but could become a raging Irish banshee when for nothing better to do I would put my head round the kitchen door and shout, " to hell with the Pope! " Katie left to be married and my sister Morag took up the house-keeping, but my father would often decide a feed was necessary and set to himself. The most nourishing of these meals was a legacy from island days called *Bonnach Gruthain*. The recipe for this most satisfying feed was head and neck of a fairly big codfish, with a kind of bannock, round and solid, made up of such things as oatmeal, chopped liver and onion, stuffed in its mouth. The whole was boiled, the water poured off, and served with or without a white sauce. I can still remember with relish the hunger-satisfying mixture of white fish and " cod haggis ". Many an extra yard it must have carried me in a forward rush on the rugby field.

We did many things together, my father and I. There were the fishing expeditions of glorious memory, trawling for saithe, lythe and mackerel off the Corran Rock in Loch Long, with Ardkinglas, the height of the grey head, towering above us. Ashore, we would make a fire on a shelving grey rock by a tumbling little stream to fry our fish and boil the kettle. Before my day, my father, along with the Rev. Hector Cameron, had christened it the Rock of the Psalms, laboriously carving with a piece of flintstone in big letters on the rock, *Carraig nan Salm*. Father told me how they had stood on the rock and sung a Gaelic psalm to the hills and waters of Loch Long : *Mo shuilean togam suas a chum nam beann on tig mo neart,* I to the hills will lift mine eyes, from whence doth come mine aid. We renewed the lettering every time we returned at intervals of six months or a year, and I have continued the ritual when fishing there with my own sons.

In kindly Gaelic and English letters, I received much father-to-son advice. " And so you have been at a show ", he wrote once after I had described some society function I had attended, " for heaven's sake do not let the remotest idea of the inferiority trouble get possession of your mind or soul or you are a gone coon. Generals be hanged ! Common as candlesticks ! You have a famous gift worth in lucre thousands upon thousands. You are used to it so you do not realise it, and it is well to have no cerebral swelling, but there it is as a matter of cold fact and you have a future, God willing, that no one can foresee in its fullness. The future will provide advantages you think beyond the range of the possible in your present state of mind and finances. Bide a wee — you are very young until you turn thirty ".

In one of his Gaelic letters my father wrote : " Each task your hand finds to do, do it with all your strength and purpose. That is the biggest difference between the man of no repute and the man of worth ".

My father's style had an ease and flow both in Gaelic and English which bore out his own advice to me that " simple, sensible, sincere and suitable words freely and enthusiastically expressed always get there ". His comments even on everyday things were worth reading, such as this description of the wildlife outside the window of Morag's house overlooking the Gareloch : " This week is about in — or is it 'out'? — and I must report progress. Summer is coming gradually, tardily. One day like yesterday there is no doubt about it, but today we are back to early spring again, coldish winds and cloudy sky. The swallows have not come en masse yet, but other birds seem to be very busy domestically. There is a swarm of starlings nesting above our southern attic window. There is a hole under the eaves there that lets them in below the roof. They are Socialists, Communists, for they all go in by the same hole and from the constant chatter of young and old are apparently having the same amount of say in things. I take it that the government is a Soviet one. Although my robin tenants have been eaten out by the dirty rats I have a round dozen other families getting on nicely about the house. The plovers are not happy, whatever is bothering them. I can see from their scooping sometimes that an alien of some sort is in their midst. The first nest we found is now deserted, eggs and all. I can never make sure of finding the other one. Maybe it has been harrowed. My apple and pear trees recently planted are in leaf and the rhoddies promise to come out soon — I took a young sapling of a rowan tree from the hill the other day and planted it opposite the one at the south gate. Jean MacIntyre's superannuated mare came along shortly afterwards, put her head over the hedge and made a meal of the delicacy. It looks now as if I had planted a bare walking stick . . . "

My father, as president of An Comunn, spent much time travelling to provincial Mods. I have a letter in which he describes a humorous incident on the way to a Mod at Strontian :

" I and Neil were for the first night in the big house of Ardgour. Warm-hearted is the man himself and kindly his wife. This is where the generous house is and every possible thing done in style as though we were dukes.

" It was from Glasgow I had left and Morag handed me my case when we stopped at Arrochar.* I had never looked to see what was in it or what was not in it, but I knew I had put in many

* John Bannerman senior and Morag had their home at Arrochar at that time.

little things — studs and tacks for my boots and oh, there is no knowing what else I myself had put in the case before I went to Glasgow for a meeting. When we reached Ardgour a servant maid took the case from me and went up the stairs with it. There was nothing to do but let it go. We had a tremendous dinner — right to the finger bowls! We strolled through the beautiful parks that surrounded the house and eventually it came time to go to bed. I was told I would find my room easily, that my clothes were laid out, but he himself [Ardgour] came up with us. We looked in at one of the doors but Neil did not recognise the pyjamas as his. We looked in on another room and I had no certain knowledge that the pyjamas on the bed were mine. It was after that that I saw my case and knew that this was my room — but when I looked inside the case, bless me if everything that had been in it had been taken out and I did not know where they had been put!

" ' Are these your things? ' said Ardgour, pulling out a drawer. I did not know whether they were or not but nevertheless I said they were and the situation was then in order. There were the clean clothes that Morag put in — shirts and semmits [vests], another pair of pyjamas, all put away in separate drawers, and the collars where they ought to be, and every pen and paper and the rest put in different places. Daft work when I was not to be in the house but one night. By Jove, we laughed about the whole business. Fortunately Neil's case was locked, otherwise the same thing would have happened to him. He said that it was Providence that saved him for it was no better than a rag store of every kind that was in his case.

" We had a splendid Mod in the new ' tin ' hall they have now at Strontian . . . "

My father made a good president of An Comunn. His knowledge of Gaelic song was exhaustive and he was responsible for bringing to national and provincial Mods many old songs which might otherwise have been lost. He was himself able to add to the words and music of incomplete old songs and make them available again. He composed many songs and collaborated with the late Sir Hugh Roberton in a number of his publications. In contrast to my father's experience as a playwright — which I shall describe later — Sir Hugh insisted he got credit for his contributions. The song *Come along, come along, let us foot it out together,* for which my father composed the music, has circled the world.

The music for *Westering Home,* another favourite of Roberton's famous Orpheus Choir, was also composed by Bannerman's father. Bannerman senior taught his son many of the songs he saved from oblivion. " I got one or two new songs while I was away, three of them from a man Morrison belonging to Mull ", he wrote from Tiree where he was attending a Mod. Bannerman later used some of them in his ceilidh programmes on television.

My father's wit in speech and writing was appreciated among a wide Gaelic public. A series of articles he wrote in Gaelic on Gaelic proverbs for the *Highland Monthly* magazine, long defunct, are accounted models of their kind.

But much of his work has remained unrecognised to this day. This was the lifetime of Gaelic plays and dialogues, forerunners of the emergent Gaelic drama movement, which my father wrote but for which no credit came to him because they were published and performed in his brother-in-law's name. *Mairead Og,* a three-act Gaelic play dictated to my Uncle Archie by my father won the £100 prize awarded in the early 'twenties by An Comunn, but it was presented in Uncle Archie's name. They split the prize between them. I do not blame my uncle, a kindly soul with little dundreary whiskers, for the deception grew from small beginnings when my father first wrote lectures for Uncle Archie to deliver to the Gaelic Ceilidh. Year after year from 1890 onwards my father had to write a serious, academic address for his own annual lecture to the ceilidh, while he also wrote a humorous one for my uncle to deliver.

I have today a tin trunk full of scripts of Gaelic plays, dialogues and lectures written in my uncle's careful Victorian longhand, to which I fortuitously fell heir when his widow, my Aunt Maggie, died. All of them have corrections in my father's hand. Not only did he dictate the material but he also had to spell out many of the Gaelic words, and correct again later. My uncle was neither fluent nor accurate in spoken or written Gaelic and he could not keep up with my father's dictation. I knew this at first hand as I was sometimes in the room doing school homework when the farce was proceeding. Often the words had to be altered from those father would naturally use to suit my uncle's Argyll intonation and background. Any incipient juvenile criticism of these pro-ceeding was stifled by my uncle's habit of always arriving at our

home with a little poke of apple tarts which my sister Morag and
I devoured. We therefore welcomed these frequent visits.

Uncle Archie was a heavy pipe smoker, and when visiting his
house in Gourock I gazed with awe at the great reserve of pipes
of all shapes and sizes he had acquired. I can still see a magnificent
yellow meerschaum pipe reclining on the rack, king of all the lesser
pipes drawn up in serried rows beside him. King Meerschaum had
a proud shape like the prow of a Viking ship — a majestic sight
with smoke issuing from the bowl which was protected by a hinged
brass perforated lid. It was with rapt attention, too, that I used
to sit watching Uncle drink his morning tea out of a huge, multi-
coloured breakfast cup. This had a china lip inside which kept his
straggly moustache from swishing in the tea as he drank. The
device was not entirely effective, for after each mouthful his lower
lip would come up and wring the last drops from the bedraggled
ends of his moustache. As a droll, Victorian kind of figure, I had
a great affection for him.

I tell the story of this collaboration now because there is none
living who can be hurt by the truth. There was no obligation on
my father to continue this self-sacrifice. Perhaps if these works of
his are ever published his wit and scholarship in written Gaelic
will be more widely appreciated. I would not infer that literature
suffered a great loss because of my father's self-effacement, but on
his own small canvas of life he showed a high notion of the rule
of right and the eternal fitness of things. In mitigation of my uncle's
part I would give you my father's answer when asked why he
had agreed to it. Characteristically he claimed no exalted self-
sacrifice. His anwer was : " Once started, I was forced to go on.
I'm not sure that I would have done the work for myself ". Perhaps,
however, modesty dictated the answer.

3

GROWING UP IN TWO WORLDS

EVERYTHING conspired to make my life one of two worlds — the exhilarating, materialistic Lowland life of Glasgow, which I came to love, and the other, softer, timeless Celtic world shot through with the traditions of a thousand years.

My love of Glasgow and its people has, because of my upbringing, a deep Celtic root. I suggest that the roots transplanted from the soil of Gaeldom and set deep in the dark, crowded streets yielded sap that strengthened the Glasgow tree.

From the clean air and green straths of the Highlands the refugees from economic ills and persecution swarmed into the poorer areas and the slums of Glasgow. They had little of the world's goods in their native straths, and that which they had, had been destroyed. Were they lucky enough to have voyaged to Oban or the Clyde from the islands by brown-sailed smack, then a few sticks of furniture might have been brought with them to found a new home. But hard cash was not plentiful. They settled down with the help of friends who rallied round in time of need as when *aig an tigh,* at home in the township.

What a bulwark against the degrading influences of poverty and overcrowding were the faith, traditions and the Gaelic language of Highland immigrants! In the midst of the Glasgow slums their homes were little islands of proud and civilised living. When the door closed on the noisome filth of their surroundings the kitchen with its *dreasair,* or old-fashioned sideboard with shelves stacked with cups and plates and shining "wally dugs", was again part of the thatched cottage nestling in the curve of the hillside. Outside the undertones of a great city might be the *ataireachd ard,* the sound of the swelling sea. Missing only was the peat fire flame and the heart-scent from it.

The Highlander was soon to be the backbone of many trades and professions, including the Glasgow police. Glasgow's hospitals echoed to the Gaelic voices of the Highland girls, and those who didn't become nurses went into domestic service and were a godsend to the chatelaines of the big houses "away up in Kelvinside". I have seen the domestic quarters of some of these now old houses, and the ladder up which the Highland maid had to climb to her box above the kitchen must have reminded her of the ladder to the hay loft in the old barn at home.

Gaelic was the language of my home, church, lectures, picnics and holidays. It was the language of song, too, for I was in the St. Columba Church junior choir under A. B. Ferguson. "A.B." was a splendid example of the Argyll Gael, a native of the Cowal district who worked in a Glasgow engineering shop and had two loves : first, shinty, and second, Gaelic music. He made for me a beautiful little shinty stick and told me he thought I'd make a better shinty player than a Gaelic singer.

At that time we lived overlooking the Moray Park in Shawlands — now built over — and the first refereed games I saw were of shinty, played on a pitch there which I have always associated with the Glasgow Skye shinty team. After a game the players used to crowd into our dining room, and injured men often used to have their wounds bathed in the house. There was a wooden shack set some distance from the pitch, so small that it looked as if half a dozen men would fill it. I was fascinated to see twenty-four men come out of it after changing for their game — not that they ever apparently did much changing. The teams would appear in all kinds of garb with, as a rule but not always, a team jersey. The Skye, I remember, had a kind of Queen's Park-striped jersey and the famous Kaid MacLean (named after a general who had seen service in north Africa) playing at full back or in goal wore a sort of velvet rugby cap with a swinging tassel and sometimes long trousers tucked into his football boots. One Saturday at a Kyle v. Skye game I saw Donald McCorquodale, whose brother Hugh was "Fingal", the Glasgow reporter of the *Oban Times,* running along the touchline with a bunch of shinty sticks under his arm. Donald's burden rapidly diminished as the sticks of his team shattered under fierce tackling. There was one little Skye man on the wing, a particular thorn in the flesh of Kyle, who wore a fisherman's cap with a glossy skip. Donald was exhorting his team, and finally exasperated by the success of the little Skye man, shouted in despair to his team, "Will ye no' watch that bloody admiral !"

It was in Moray Park that I flew my kite until it disappeared into the clouds over the church spires of Queen's Park, and where

I would tie a piece of bread to each end of a length of string and watch the duel of two seagulls flying along linked by the string, until they realised that they could only end their partnership by spewing out what remained of the bread — fun for me at least. There were other fights between the green linties and greedy starlings over crumbs in our window box.

Well remembered too were the many walks I took with my father around Shawlands before I was word perfect in the Gaelic speech I had to make at the opening of the great 1911 Exhibition in Glasgow. I can still feel how sick I was when I made that speech, perhaps of two minutes' duration, while making a presentation to Lady Cassilis in *An Clachan,* the Highland village. But I loved the thatched cottages of *An Clachan* and the old Highland lady busily carding wool and spinning by the door, just as I was entranced by the African villages close by. I was fascinated by the bizarre costumes of the natives, by the bangles on their arms, the rings on their noses, and by their chatter, wild singing and the rapid tattoo of their long black fingers on the skin drums. It was only in later life that I came to condemn the patronising spirit behind the spectacle; one colonial, the other Highland, one three thousand miles distant, the other less than three hundred miles away. In one was the black boy, in the other the Highland " ghillie " (even the accepted spelling of the word ghillie in English connotes something contemptuous, for *gille* is the correct Gaelic spelling of the word meaning boy). Both villages had the attraction of the primitive for " civilised " observers.

Any prowess I acquired in soccer was nurtured in Moray Park. Of my schooling I have this to say : Shawlands Academy till the age of thirteen set me up in soccer, Glasgow High School from then until eighteen set me up in rugby. Wee Mr. Allan in Shawlands had my gratitude for teaching me soccer and a very little general knowledge, Mr. Ellicot in the High School for teaching me rugby and a very little French. Above all, I respected Dr. Peter Pinkerton, Rector of the High School in my time — a little man, like my father, but immense in his possession of humane and intellectual qualities.

Playground football, with a ball that could vary from a tennis ball to a tin can, was just one of the unorganised seasonal games I delighted in, like moshie and conkers and the strenuous relieve-o. Moshie was played on an area of hard-packed ashes outside Shawlands Academy playground. We cherished our capital of " bools " (marbles) and added to it with the acquisitive glee of any tycoon. The span of the finger and thumb was high ritual on the dirty ground to get you nearer the moshie hole. Great accuracy was required for another form of competitive bools where you aimed with a big " jorie " from about six feet distance, balancing on legs set wide apart, at a hole full of bools belonging to all the players. The more accurate and forceful your shot, the more bools you dislodged. These were added to your stock. In one variation of the game you started off about fifty feet away from the hole. You threw the jorie high into the air and as far forward as you dared, attempting to catch it in a variety of awkward postures — hand extended behind your back or curled behind your leg. You were allowed a shot at the bools in the hole from the spot at which you caught the jorie. How jacket pockets sagged and suffered after a successful moshie evening! Success in conkers was equally rewarding, for to have the champion conker in school or district was equivalent to owning a Lonsdale Belt, and challengers turned up from far and near.

During the school holidays I was sent " home " each year to the croft farm of Ardreas at Caolas on the Isle of Tiree, run by cousins of my father. There I would spend idyllic days on the machair, riding bareback on the Highland ponies or bathing and fishing in the Port Ban, the little harbour. I would speak Gaelic the day long to the old man of the farm whom we all called Grandfather, to *Gill-easbuig* the man of all work, and to Flora, a middle-aged aunt skilled in every aspect of house and farm work. Her girdle scones and great round bannocks of oatcake melted in the mouth.

Once when my father came to collect me from Tiree at the end of the holiday we sailed home round the stormy Mull of Kintyre, munching Machair Farm oatcakes and cold chicken on the windy, rainswept deck. There was no room round the one small table in the saloon which seemed only big enough to seat the officers of the ship. In those days the MacBrayne line didn't make much distinction between human and animal passengers — though however inhospitable conditions on MacBrayne ships were in those days, there was always the kindly Highland welcome from skipper and crew for the humblest of their passengers. I am not sure but that stots and ewes got preference in accommodation, at least below deck. Up on deck the human passengers had more room, for after all, MacBraynes knew *we* wouldn't jump overboard.

Some voyages on stormy nights over the Minch stamped themselves on my mind as reminiscent of the terrible scenes I had read about on the emigrant ships to Canada. The MacBrayne ship, crowded with women and children returning to Glasgow after the Fair holiday, could well have been one of those emigrant ships : outside the wind howling, the ship rolling and pitching, creaking and groaning; below deck the dim lights just visible in the murky oil-laden atmosphere, the engines clanking and thudding away for dear life and human beings sprawled everywhere, sickness mingling with the oil and water in the scuppers, the squawling baby clutched lovingly to the mother's bosom — a mother whose face was white and sickly, her hair straggling hopelessly as she tried to pacify her other tired and restless children. What a price to pay for a few days " at home "! But every year it would be the same. No hardship on the voyage would keep the exiles from breathing again, even for a few days, the clean air of their beloved homeland. Bitter resentment stirred in me as I witnessed the shortcomings of this so-called transport service over the years.

But for a boy, those were halcyon days in the Isle of Tiree, and I found plenty of ways to amuse myself — like the making of *giollan-gaoithe*, the light-as-a-feather toy made by generations of children in the Hebrides. What a dance it led me, and to what an ignominious end. Stealthily I braved the dark recesses of the stable to creep up on the brown hen that Flora said had laid every egg of her long life in the corner of the treviss. Then, clutching fiercely, I seized some of her wing feathers in my fingers and tugged them out as she ran screeching through the broken skylight. The next step was to stand on tiptoe on Grandfather's armchair, just managing to reach with my free hand the whisky bottle on the second top shelf of the kitchen cupboard. Luckily the cork hadn't been pushed tightly home or Flora, returning from the milk closet where her great pans of milk gathered their yellow head of cream, would have surprised her young visitor apparently coveting Machair Farm's symbol of hospitality. But it was the cork I wanted, not the whisky. Once I had extracted it I had the raw materials complete, and it was not long before I had proudly constructed my first toy. The process was simple : merely to stick the quills firmly all round the cork in a cluster, as the grey-bearded Gilleasbuig had been at pains to show me. No toy from a shop ever held half the mischief or delight that was in *giollan-gaoithe*, this crude fly-in-the-wind.

And how it flew! I can see myself clearly as though it were yesterday — bare legs spread, chest heaving, eyeing the toy of my own creating with baleful glare. There it was, perched just out of reach on the whiskery edge of a sandy hummock, swaying to and fro on its feathery legs in the fitful summer breeze. My homespun kilt, frayed and worn, was twisted and hanging half off. Nothing must interfere with the capture of this will-o'-the-wisp, but how to do it? Fly-in-the-wind had made me run as never before. I edged up, crab-like, then plunged — but fly-in-the-wind jumped suddenly away from her anchor of bent grass stalks and danced blithely away on her feather legs. With as near a roar as I could muster I charged after her, my kilt a banner in the breeze. Down the incline she flew, over dip and hump in the direction of the rough stone byre roofed with black felt, which housed the cows and followers that were the stock of Machair's forty acres of arable and rough grassland. Foul intent was in that toy, for she made straight for the *dunan,* the dung heap or midden heaped beside the old upturned boat set on drystone walls which acted as a roof for Machair's one pig — the boat snuggling by the near wall of the byre like a chick beside its mother. Up the side of the midden danced fly-in-the-wind, only to be trapped by the fresh manure emptied that morning by Gill-easbuig. Her feather legs lost their lightness and she stuck fast.

Down the incline I charged like my ancestors in Lowland foray. Unable to stop, I splashed gloriously into the *dunan,* to be almost buried in that morning's addition to the heap — with neither straw nor rashes of winter-time bedding to cushion me. But if my body was spread out, so was my arm — five fingers triumphantly clutched the feather legs. I had her, but at what a price. With a sucking noise, the heap let us go. My pouched hand rubbed the muck that clogged my eyes and plastered my face and chest. Blue guernsey was now the same colour as grey homespun kilt — a dark and soggy brown. Still half blinded, I floundered out, and my first glance at the world around was cast fearfully towards the farm house. No one appeared from the cottage some fifty yards away, so at least neither Flora nor Grandfather had seen my dive into the muck.

" You'll be the young visitor from Glasgow, I suppose ", said a voice from behind with a chuckle.

I wheeled quickly.

" Or will you be the spirit of the *dunan* come to welcome home the cows to the milking? Eh, but you are brown mess ! "

The big-booted man continued without waiting for an answer, his eyes twinkling in the grey whiskery expanse of his face. It was the odd-job man, Gill-easbuig.

" It's certain Flora will have to look twice to find *Seonaidh beag,* wee Johnny ", he said, and then growled at the collie dog as shaggy as himself, waving his hand in the direction of a white Highland cow which had lagged far behind the others, as the cattle made their way slowly in single file along the fence that divided the fields from the rough grazing on the machair. Then Gill-easbuig turned again to me, a forlorn figure in the ruin of a kilt.

" Don't you move *A laochain,* little hero ", he said. " I'll get the cows in and tie them up and then you and me will see what can be done before Flora wonders who the tinkers have brought her ".

I tried to show gratitude, though my smile must have been a bit crooked under its crust of drying manure. I now stood at the low door of the pig house, out of sight of Flora in the farm house. The cows picked their way past me, their wide-sweeping horns lowered and canted to the side to enable them to enter the byre door. Inside I could hear the clanking of chains as Gill-easbuig tied them by the head. Soon he was back outside, and together, my hand clasped in his gnarled fist, we made our way up the hill.

" We'll make it past the kitchen ", whispered Gill-easbuig as we hesitated wondering whether to slink through the side door past the the milk closet where Flora was, or round the corner past the kitchen window. Grandfather would be sitting in his round wooden armchair by the peat fire, his shepherd's crook in his right hand and planted firmly on the stone floor, and his pipe stuck in the yellow-stained depression in his white beard. He might see Gill-easbuig passing, but by bending double I would escape detection. Grandfather could see most things with his eighty-year-old eyes, but even he could not see through the four feet of stone wall that made the cottage kitchen a cool, refreshing place when the sun blazed from the blue summer skies and a haven of warmth and peace when the Atlantic winter blast screamed above the roar of the sea on *Sgeir nan Eun,* the Reef of the Birds.

My guilty conscience about the hen made me cast a quick glance at the farm house door as we slipped past the front of the cottage. Was one of the Rhode Islands clucking around the door minus a few feathers? They often advanced cheekily right into the kitchen, when Grandfather — steel spectacles in his free hand, the big family Bible on his knee — would shoo them out with voice and stick and quite un-Christian vehemence. But the harried hen was not to be seen. We passed the window of the ben (or best room) to the point where the white-limed wall of the house merged with the coarsely-pointed black stone of the stable. At the join stood a large black barrel set firmly on a pedestal of stone, into which two gutters suspended from the eaves by fencing wire emptied summer shower and winter downpour. More than once I had just escaped a ducking in this barrel as I leaned over trying to follow the course of the pebbles I dropped into its black depths. This was what Gill-easbuig was making for. A stable brush and a pail served as the initial cleaning instruments, and slowly my kilt and guernsey began to emerge under the brushing as separate articles of clothing. Wet and dripping they might be, but at least the solid traces of the *dunan* were being removed.

"There now", said Gill-easbuig finally, "I must hurry to the byre to help Flora or she'll be asking me questions, and what would I say then?"

Bedraggled, face shining from the splashing I'd got, I held up fly-in-the-wind cheerfully. "Will I wash *giollan-gaoithe* — her legs are so dirty?"

"Aye, just do that", answered Gill-easbuig benignly, "but see you don't fall into the barrel".

By standing tiptoe on the stone platform and stretching full out I could just reach the surface of the water. "I'll dry you now", I said, eyeing the forlorn-looking toy a little dubiously, adding as an afterthought, "if Grandfather allows me near the fire".

Grandfather raised his keen old eyes from the Book and looked me over in astonishment, puffing explosively through his beard. I approached hesitantly, leaving a wet track on the grey flag-stoned floor of the kitchen.

"Bless me", he growled at last, "now if you've been to the Port Ban . . ."

It would have been a crime to go down to the little harbour alone. But before the threat could be uttered I broke in, "No, Grandfather, I've just been to the barrel. Gill-easbuig has been washing me — I fell into the *dunan*".

I held up fly-in-the-wind. "Can I dry her feet?" I asked.

Grandfather, his alarm over, sank back in his chair again. His belly, where waistcoat and blue guernsey did not quite meet trouser tops, quivered with suppressed laughter.

"Indeed you had better", he said, "and you had better dry yourself first or Flora will have something to say to you".

The old man put on his steel spectacles again and took up the Book. Once again the ticking of the clock was the only sound in the kitchen, lit by the glow of the peat fire and the glint of a sunbeam on the shining ware on the *dreasair*. It was a place where old age could sit and dream, and youth dry its tears.

Down by the shore, ceilidhs were held in the thatched cottage belonging to Lachainn MacFadyen, the old kelp fisherman. For me, these meant a frantic scurry to be home by ten o'clock, the zero hour set by Gill-easbuig. Stealthily I would creep into the kitchen to take a bowl of leathery porridge from the oven, marvelling at its bouncy quality when probed with a finger. Then I would whisper to Spot the collie dog, sitting with his ears cocked below the wooden bench, and watch with delight as he golloped the porridge, saving me from having to eat it. Off then on tiptoe to the ben room, lighted candle held high, eerie shadows guiding me to the haven of the great mountainous-bolstered bed. Sleep and breath to blow out the candle were as one.

4

INTERLUDE: AN ISLAND CEILIDH

CEILIDHS were crowded, friendly gatherings in the ceilidh house (or houses) which were a feature of every township. Old and young would meet there in the long winter evenings to sing songs, tell folk tales and sometimes to dance. They were, in a way, the evening classes of the Highlands. Now, unfortunately, they are no longer a spontaneous part of life in many Highland communities.

Let me tell you of a typical island ceilidh . . .

Lachainn MacFadyen's house, nestling in a hollow above *Bagh nan Coilleagan*, the Bay of the Shells, was like an upturned white seashell itself. Below were the million shining white shells which gave the bay its name, although it had come to be called simply Lachainn's Bay by the people who slipped and stumbled in the dark winter evenings to reach their favourite ceilidh house. Only the oldest could remember when anyone but Lachainn had stayed in the squat little dwelling, and though Lachainns were not scarce on the island, Lachainn's House was the only description required to tell where a traveller was bound of an evening.

I see Gill-easbuig from the Machair Farm carefully rounding the gable end of Kate's shop by the ferry, knowing that he is heading in the right direction in the darkness of a cold February night when his heavy boots feel the smooth well-worn path. His eyes just discern the faint line of the sand dune which shelters Lachainn's house. Cautiously he climbs over, down to level ground broken by dark hummocks of tufted grass and on to the little gate, a white blur in the darkness. The gate and the two-foot fence of pointed stobs are more ornamental than useful. They make a frame in which sits Lachainn's beehive-shaped house, straw-thatched, its thick lime-whitened walls on either side of the " sneckit " door bulging out dimly in the darkness like a welcoming bosom. Through the little gate . . . then Gill-easbuig's boots crunch on the shingle path bordered by the biggest and choicest shells from the bay below. He can hear the voice of a girl raised in the slow, sad exile's song *Caol Muile,* the Sound of Mull.

The wind wafts cold over the sound, the black hills merging with the dark mass of snow cloud to the north. The waters of the sound lap the shore in time with the sad rhythm of the age-old tune :

> *Caol Muile mo ghraidh*
> *Dan d'thug mise baigh*
> *Sann duit bheir mi gradh rim'bheo.*

> Sound of Mull, my love,
> I gave you my heart,
> Yours will it always be.

Gill-easbuig's big thumb bears down on the latch and he goes in. Putting his head round the half-open inner door to the kitchen, Gill-easbuig can see in the smoky atmosphere lit by a ship's lamp clamped to the wall that the room is *loma-lan,* more than full. Folk sit and squat on the floor, on seats, on the bench. Even the *dreasair,* laden with china, carries two young stalwarts, blue-jerseyed and red of face. Squeezed happily between them sits dark-eyed Eilidh Cameron of Acharsait, the singer of the song.

Lachainn *fear an tigh,* the man of the house, sits on the right of the glowing peat fire, his chair turned out a little to allow him to see all his visitors more easily. In his high-necked blue guernsey Lachainn is a squat, thick figure, his clean-shaven face round yet bony, somewhat forbidding in repose but enlivened by a wide smile that wrinkles the leathery skin and shows teeth that are still good — though his age is something over seventy. Lachainn is a bachelor with no close blood ties except for a brother in Glasgow, but his family on such nights is only limited by the four white walls of his kitchen. He has been a kelp fisherman, and before that he roamed the world in every kind of vessel, and rumour has it, had a wife in every port.

" Hang yourself on one of these ", is his laughing greeting to Gill-easbuig, pointing to the bacon hooks that protrude from the ceiling. " You will be a bit too old to sit on anybody's knee ".

Gill-easbuig, nicknamed the Minister for his pointed beard and his wise quips on the shortcomings of human kind, is welcomed on all sides through the haze of peat and tobacco smoke, and offered squeezed-up corners of seats. There is always fun when Gill-easbuig arrives.

" It's at the *dreasair* I'm looking ", he says. " Will there be room beside you, Eilidh? "

" The stool for you, sly man ", cuts in Lachainn, bending down and drawing a small three-legged stool from behind his armchair. Laughing, Gill-easbuig doubles his large frame down on the stool. Lachainn calls for a tune on the " box of music ", and from the dimness of the far corner of the kitchen bursts a melody in quadrille time, played expertly on the melodion. Fergie the young ferryman is as nimble on the keys as he is on his boat. The young tap their feet, but the night is young yet and the dance will come later when the older folk have had their songs and story and talk. Besides, the young like this part of the ceilidh as much as the old. Is not this the pleasant school? — for whether they know it or not they are gathering to themselves the wisdom and experience of their people. All is renewed in the old, and passed on to the young as easily as the milk from the breast to the child.

The tune ends. " What about *Bodach a' churachd dheirg,* the Old Man with the Red Bonnet? " says Lachainn. " *Siubhad Eoghain Posd,* Go ahead Hugh the Post ".

Hugh, with a self-conscious look on his narrow-peaked, weather-beaten face, fingers the brass buttons of his Government waistcoat and gives himself a hitch or two on his seat on the bench. A chorus of approval greets the suggestion. This is Hugh's story and his variations on the doings of the old man with the red bonnet have become famous. Hugh says neither yea nor nay. Clearing his throat, he starts with the time-honoured, " *Bha uair ann,* there was a time when . . . "

By virtue of his calling, Hugh the Post knows more about the people and their doings than most. He is general adviser on the various Government forms that are always a part of his heavy postbag. He carries the news of what is happening on the island and on the mainland, too, and if Hugh does not know the exact circumstances of an incident he will always supply them from his own lively imagination.

The old man with the red bonnet is always welcome, for Hugh serialises his adventures, and though the stories are based on old traditions he often lays the action round some local inhabitant or incident, neither difficult for his hearer to locate. This time he tells how the village boys played a well-known island prank on the *bodach* one dark night by tying his old mare to the sneck of his door, so that when he answered their knock the mare tramped on his slippered foot with an iron-shod hoof. The old man got his own back by balancing a couple of pails of icy water above the lintel and then luring the boys in. Drenched, cold and fearful of his wrath, they fled for home.

"There was not a sound from the *bodach*", says Hugh, "but if it could have been seen, the wee tassel on his red bonnet shook a little . . . "

Gill-easbuig's contribution usually consisted of telling about the emigrants he had met in every corner of the globe, and these were fascinating for those who had remained *aigh an tigh,* at home. This time he sings lustily an old Ossianic chant, his grey beard wagging fiercely as it tells how his people defied the Norse invaders.

As the hours go by the lamp above Lachainn's head grows dim in the tobacco smoke, flickering on the faces of those nearby — now sad with the pathos of a love song sung in deep, shy tones by one of the sailors on the *dreasair;* now merry as everyone laughs at the mimicry of Fergie the ferryman. Fergie can " do " the people across the sound, much to the delight of the local folk. There is much rivalry between the islands — the fishing boat regatta, the annual sports, to say nothing of the battle of wits between them. If Caolas lost the races they could always console themselves with the opinion that they were superior in mind to their neighbours.

Now at last it is Lachainn's turn, for the man of the house at a ceilidh is by tradition expected to tell a story.

"Alick the miller's son — him that left the island last year to be a railway porter at Morar — was leaning against the gates of the level-crossing when along comes a big touring car with a fancy English tourist driving it. ' Why are the gates half open, half shut ', shouts the driver angrily. ' Well it's like this, sir ', says Alick through his stutter, ' I was ha-ha-half expecting a train '."

And so it goes until it is time for the dancing.

Now and again there were unexpected guests at Lachainn's ceilidh. One night there was a scuffling on the floor in the far corner beside the *dreasair,* and two small figures were discovered on all fours, trying to hide.

"What on earth will your Mammy say to you, out at this time of the night? " says Gill-easbuig, pushing his way over to them and pointing to Lachainn's yellow-faced clock on the mantelpiece, ticking off the last few minutes before ten.

It was the two fair-haired boys of Machair Farm, my holiday playmates, shyly pressing themselves against the wall. Calum, the younger one, five years old, hangs his head — not so much at

Gill-easbuig's words but because he is shy, Iain, nearly twelve, with the same blue eyes and unruly fair curly hair, stands straighter and a little in front, as though to protect his younger brother. But his face is grave and flushed, and he looks at Gill-easbuig with a guilty expression.

"Ach, why don't you be quiet?" says Lachainn. "Leave the boys alone. I was going to send them home now anyway".

Calum's head comes up and he smiles gratefully.

"Well", says Gill-easbuig, "I'll be away up with you now to see you don't get into more mischief, but what will your Mammy say?"

"What's your hurry, Gill-easbuig?" asks Lachainn. "Can you not let the boys be? Let's hear what Iain and Calum can do in the way of a song before you go".

Gill-easbuig shakes his head doubtfully. He has taught Iain and Calum many good Gaelic songs, but it takes a chorus of approval from all sides to make him repent.

"Give them a verse or two of *Leis an Lurgain o hi*", he says at last.

The boys clasp hands and start the old boat song with its eager rowing rhythm. They make a curious contrast : Iain on the threshold of adolescence, his voice a little harsh, but pleasing, his eyes fixed on the lamp, his head slightly tilted, his fresh face flushed with embarrassment. His aim is clearly to get done as soon as possible. Calum presses close to Iain as though he would like to hide between him and the wall, his round, wholesome face framed in waving curls and turned up to his brother's, seeking inspiration and comfort in this frightening situation. Softly, gently, but with the true rowing rhythm, the brothers' voices blend in this melody of the sea — the sea whose sound is always in the ears and in the hearts of the island folk.

The boys' voices, as yet without the nasal quality that often characterises the singing of older Highland people, are clear and melodious. Neither has ever sung indoors before. A hush falls on the ceilidh folk and not even the chorus is joined. There is warmth in Gill-easbuig's heart — the many hours spent in the *iollan,* the stack yard, or out on the green knoll on the machair, have not been misspent. The boyish voices hesitatingly explore the unaccustomed ceilidh kitchen, and there is quiet in Lachainn's as the last clear notes die away. The tick of the clock is loud in the stillness until applause and stamping feet break the spell.

"Aye, Gill-easbuig ", says Lachainn with some emotion, " you've done your work well. It won't be the last time we will hear the boys sing ".

" Come on, Calum and Iain ", says Gill-easbuig gruffly. " It will be a different story when Mammy hears of this, and my grey hairs won't protect me ", he says with emphasis, amid laughter.

" *Oidhche mhath,* good night ", comes from all sides as Gill-easbuig shepherds his charges to the door. Outside, in the fitful cold light of the moon, riding low now in the scurrying clouds, they stand for a moment to get their bearings. Inside they hear the renewed laughter of the ceilidh. Gill-easbuig takes Iain's hand and with an arm round Calum's shoulder to shield him from the cold wind, they trudge up the sand dunes and over the grazing to Machair Farm.

If Gill-easbuig gives them a scolding for going to the ceilidh, it has a tuneful air that makes Iain step out and Calum trot to keep up. Quickly and light-heartedly they cover the rising ground towards the friendly, shining eye of Machair Farm kitchen. The age-old island ceilidh is over for them.

But back at the ceilidh house it will be hours yet before Lachainn turns down the wick in the misty wall lamp, and with a breathy puff brings darkness to his ceilidh kitchen. The thin gleam of the dying peat fire and the echoing sound of song and laughter guides him to the lonely bed box in the closet. But there will never be room for loneliness in Lachainn's heart, for he has the friendship of his ceilidh children. They have gone but for a few hours. They will be back.

In the sigh of the wind and the *ataireachd ard,* the song of the sea, is the faint, lilting echo of the ceilidh mouth music, carrying a promise that the soul of the Highland people will not perish while they value simple things — the things that made the blood strong and the heart kindly.

5

HIGHLAND HOLIDAYS AND HOLY DAYS

ANOTHER year and it was away over the hills and glens to my mother's people in the Isle of Skye, staying with the godly, kindly old Baptist minister, the Rev. Allan MacDougall of Harrapool, Broadford. This meant repeated walks on a Sunday to and from the long, low, white-washed church at the crossroads. There we would listen to Mr. MacDougall, so neat in his black frock coat and white bow tie, telling us in long, sonorous Gaelic phrases of the hereafter, and how insignificant was our place in the beautiful temporal world around us.

Then off on an expedition via the Kyle of Lochalsh to other relations of my mother in the *Comraich* — the Applecross peninsula — whose headlands we could see dimly across the sound from Skye. Fifty years ago the *Comraich* was the home of thousands of people where now only hundreds remain. Recent press headlines told of the possible evacuation of the remnant of five communities for lack of a road.*

There was the added thrill of sailing from Kyle along the coastline in a converted smack skippered by another cousin; of unloading meal, flour, paraffin, wire netting at the little jetty at Applecross; of stumbling over the round clean boulders fashioned by aeons of tides, up to the two-storey cottage sitting on its carpet of green sea turf; of curling up at night, tired and a bit strange, in the standard Highland soft baggy-bolstered bed in an upstairs room, the last sound in my ears the soothing sigh of the wavelets.

Then it was morning, and with it the start of Communion Week in Applecross. I stayed in the house of the chief elder, whose son became the Rev. Donald MacKinnon, an eminent divine in the Free Church of Scotland. I was to receive more concentrated

* The first section of a road into Applecross was opened in 1970.

religion in those few days than at any time in my life. Early morning seven o'clock service in the church on the headland, prayers on our knees in the kitchen morning and evening, elbows on a chair, evening service in the church on Thursday and Friday.

Every house in the village was now filling with black-coated visitors. They slept on *beingigh*, the kitchen bench, and on floor. My large bed was invaded by two grey-headed elders on the Friday night and I had to lie close against the wall, as much to avoid being tickled by their whiskers as to give them room. I learned then the meaning of the phrase " climbing the wall ".

Everyone was kindly, but grave with a due sense of the solemnity of the occasion. For me, however, there was one piece of light relief at the *ceist,* or question service in the church. Various elders or members of the congregation would stand and preach to a text. That evening an old man in the pew in front of me was holding forth, swinging his arms about vehemently. Beside him was an old lady with a cape on her shoulders like the tippet Glasgow policemen used to wear, and on her head a mutch from which protruded a big black feather. In one of his swings the elder swiped feather and hat on to the back of her neck. Had it not been tied by a ribbon under her chin it would have travelled some distance. But never a pause did he make in his declamation, and the old lady meekly set her hat straight again. Not a ripple disturbed the quiet devotion of the crowded congregation. The glossy black feather rose again as jauntily as ever in the air.

Sunday morning broke calm and fresh and clear. Looking over the sound to Skye, *Beinn-na-Caillich,* the Mountain of the Old Woman, rising behind Broadford, made a deep-blue, rounded outline against the lighter blue of the white-flecked heavens. It seemed to me as I stood on the shore in the hush of early morning, looking across to the Cuillin hills of Skye, that colour and sound — the song of the waves lapping the clean stones, the green of the sea turf, the expanse of blue sea and sky and mountain — were uniting to glorify God in his heaven, and that through nature's beauty He was giving His people a fitting frame for their Sunday morning worship. The white-washed cottages by the shore, each with its complement of worshippers, were as much a part of the spellbinding beauty of the scene as the dazzling white seagulls, dotted motionless on rock and islet.

Then the boats from nearby communities started to arrive, brown-sailed smacks, motor fishing vessels and even rowing boats. The bigger ones were black with people standing on the decks.

Nosing their way into the bay, small silver waves curling at their bows, the crowded boats were truly a flotilla of righteousness.

The little church on the headland could not hope to contain the invasion, so at eleven o'clock the scene was set on the hill among the bracken. Five or six hundred people ranged themselves in tiers as in an amphitheatre, and on the level ground below us was the white-clothed communion table. It held at one sitting only thirty or forty people. They came to the table in relays — indeed a marathon service.

In addition to the faithful gathered together on that hillside there were millions of little winged devils which became more voracious as the afternoon wore on. My kilt was no protection against the Highland midge, and my attention was sadly diverted from the saving grace of the preacher's words. There seemed to be many preachers and many sermons, and an interminable renewal of the complement at the communion table (though not all the congregation counted themselves worthy of taking the sacrament). The midges seemed to mobilise their multitudes against me alone, for as far as I could see no one in the vast gathering even surreptitiously scratched himself. All kept their attention, solemn and immovable, on the preacher. The theory of acclimatisation was amply demonstrated for me that day. Raised in Glasgow, my skin (whatever my blood) was not West Highland. It was a relief when we started to sing, for I could move my head and stretch my neck at the high notes. It was also a relief to pray, for then we stood up, and I could move and deal death to some of the midges.

What a glorious wealth of joyful sound rose triumphantly into the blue sky. The bearded precentor, who led the psalm singing, stood by the communion table giving out the line, his voice full of melody and graceful inflection, with a faintly nasal quality not accounted musical by the purists but pleasing to me because of the folk quality of the sound. At the end of each line he seemed to smack his lips as though tasting the sweetness of words and music. No symphony could compare with the wild, natural swelling cadences of the psalm tunes Coleshill and Martyrdom, sung by these devout people in this setting. Prayers were lengthy, sonorous and earnest, and sighs of assent and groans of remorse rose from the congregation. At last it was all over. The crowd spread down the hillside like a black river in flood to the white houses by the shore, where the miracle of feeding them among the families of the township would begin.

Economic and social changes have blotted out even in my generation such scenes of communal worship, except perhaps here and there in the Western Isles or the north-west mainland. The people of Gaeldom have continued to scatter to other lands in the past half-century, as in the century before, and in the modern world, science and technology have wiped the slate clean of simple things. That gathering by the sea of the Hebrides seems as remote today as another by the Sea of Galilee, yet barely half a century has passed since the " flotilla of righteousness " set sail for home.

In those days people were still thick on the ground in certain parts of the Highlands. Their religion was strict and accounted narrow by the standards of the south, and condemned by the humanist as a hindrance to economic and material progress. But at least in those days, though the tenets were tough, religious observance was based on concern for one's neighbour. The community would assist anyone whose work on the croft was behind or who needed help in illness or other misfortune. So while the individual had a narrow but sincere concern for his personal relations with his God, he also based his faith on the Christian precept " Love thy neighbour as thyself ".

Times have changed. Symbolic of the old days was the cup of tea and the girdle scone smothered in rich butter and creamy crowdie, given freely to the stranger at the door, given with a blessing and no thought of payment. Many a hard-bitten tourist was ecstatic about the Highlander's lack of selfish, materialistic outlook. Today that tourist resentfully deplores the change. The bed-and-breakfast notice is the sign of the advance of materialism into the Highlands. In entering the rat race, the Highlander has lost his communal spirit, and rivalry replaces neighbourliness.

6

A LITTLE LEARNING

DURING the summer months I used to help with my fees for Glasgow University by working as an inspector for the Department of Agriculture, grading the potato crops growing throughout Scotland. I learned to recognise by the haulms alone about two hundred different types of potato. And then before I left for Oxford I spent nearly a year as assistant to the famous Donald MacKelvie, potato king of the beautiful Isle of Arran — and for that matter, of Britain. Throughout the bleak, cold mornings of January and February I used to make my way, at 7.30 in the dark before the dawning, down the rocky foreshore in front of his house in Lamlash to dip hastily in what was an Arctic sea. All this was because Mr. MacKelvie had disciplined himself in the same way until he was well up in years, and because he considered it to be good training for the rugby Internationals I played in those years. It was good to get back and sit at the most heavily-laden breakfast table I have ever seen, and to win MacKelvie's quiet approving smile when he returned from his early morning visit to his bakery and grocery business in Lamlash.

Was it because I followed his advice and example in this way that he named his famous potato Arran Banner after me? I like to think it was because I saved the variety from being lost in a mixture of closely allied seed. Arran Banner was at that stage just a number, nearly at the end of its trials in field plots in Arran. I had to examine these plots minutely for any signs of disease or mutation. In what was to be Arran Banner I discovered some plants with a difference in depth of colouration at the leaf base, and a ribbing on the main stem, indistinguishable except after prolonged scrutiny. The offending plants were removed after much deliberation, and Arran Banner eventually won the gold medal for a new variety and became one of the biggest area maincrops in Britain. Its chief fault was that it grew too big if well done to, but would give quality and yield if grown without pampering. Perhaps there is a moral in that.

43

MacKelvie's work over nearly half a century affected permanent improvement in the standard and quality of the potato and its cultivation, widening its horizon as a cash and food crop at home and abroad. His industry and precision were phenomenal, from the stage when he cross-fertilised the flower to the placing of about two hundred seeds of the " plum " on to a dampened sheet of white blotting paper. From then on he would carry the produce of many different plums represented by thousand of brother-and-sister potatoes through rigorous tests, discarding ruthlessly in the subsequent years until he might have only five or six left to go on field trial — all of which might fail in the final tests.

Whatever Donald MacKelvie tackled he was never satisfied with less than the best. His breeding of Highland ponies produced a superlative quality and grace, attained perhaps by sacrificing a little of the ruggedness demanded by the crofter in his work horse. MacKelvie rode his three-speed bicycle to and from his house to his shop, summer and winter, disdaining the use of a car, although he was troubled badly by a lame leg that sometimes pained him greatly. His pockets were always full of loaf sugar, and his ponies, broken and unbroken, never needed calling when they saw him.

I was so busy at Glasgow High School as a prefect and captain of the school that my Highers suffered and I had to sit a number of prelim exams to enable me to enter Glasgow University. Those were the days of freedom in learning — no axing of the immature or unsuccessful at 11-plus in school or at 20-plus in the university. I accumulated eight or nine professional exams to sit in 1926, my last year at Glasgow University, having been very busy playing rugby and enjoying the social life. In order to work without interruption I left my home and took digs at the top of a tenement overlooking Kelvingrove Park. I have never seen so many consecutive sunrises as during that six-month period. But miraculously I graduated M.A., B.Sc. in Agriculture in record time. I am sure this was due to the extra kindnesses of various professors, chief amongst whom was the kindly and erudite Professor George Henderson of Chemistry, and his lab demonstrators, the much-beloved Mary Andross and Jean Paterson. Exams and International matches were seldom allowed to clash, and if they did I played the International and sat a special examination later. Those were spacious days! But it was not all just luck and goodwill — working till sunrise also contributed to the successful outcome.

In 1927 I took up a post-graduate scholarship course in Agricultural Economics at Balliol College, Oxford, into whose august and scholarly surroundings I was admitted, I suspect, not wholly on intellectual grounds. I am grateful for my sojourn there. Oxford or Cambridge can do little to make a Scotsman forget his traditions if he has previously been grounded at a Scottish school and university. It is those Scotsmen who are sent as youngsters to an English prep school and on to Eton or Harrow and then Oxford or Cambridge who finally emerge as little Englishmen — more English sometimes than the English.

Oxford was generous and enlightening to me. There I met men like John Maxton, a great agricultural economist and brother of Jimmy Maxton, M.P., whom we visited together many times in the flat in Battersea he shared with his fellow members of the Independent Labour Party at Westminster, Geordie Buchanan and the Rev. Campbell Stephen. They were true Scottish rebels whose Socialism had the needs of Scotland as its base and the cruel unemployment of Clydeside in the 'thirties as its spur. The three Clydeside M.P.s had a real division and economy of labour in the kitchen-cum-sitting room of their flat, where movement was reduced to a minimum. Their dining table was placed as near as possible to the stove to allow Geordie Buchanan, who was the cook, to sit in his chair while he made the fry, and then swing round to distribute the result round the table. It was Jimmy Maxton's task to set the table with dishes and cutlery from a cupboard placed conveniently close to *his* chair. Campbell Stephen, sitting with his back to the sink, had no trouble in dousing the dishes when their repast was over.

These three endearing Scots musketeers showed supreme indifference, outwardly at least, for the magnificence of their surroundings at Westminster. Amidst the statues of famous men and the panoply of English history, it was as if they took off their jackets, rolled up their sleeves and laid about them — and the shibboleths of Westminster toppled before their onslaught. To them, even the Labour Party was but part of the dead weight of the reactionary Establishment. The Independent Labour Party which they helped to form was never to prosper, remaining a splinter group, but I am sure Keir Hardie would have approved their uncompromising fight to better the state of Scotland, and particularly to relieve the misery of their unemployed fellows.

Even while at Oxford I was concerned with the survival and development of the Gaelic language. Another enthusiast was

Aonghas Mor, Big Angus, the Marquis of Graham,* who was six feet four inches in height and a heavyweight boxing blue. He and I, along with John Lorne Campbell of Canna, were responsible for starting the first extra-mural class in Scottish Gaelic ever to be held, as far as I am aware, in Oxford. We went together to Jesus College and asked Professor John Fraser of the chair of Celtic if he would conduct a class in which we could read such books as *Caraid nan Gaidheal,* Friend of the Gael, by Dr. Norman Macleod.†

I was astonished by Professor Fraser's reaction. He enquired if we were doing this out of sentimental regard for Gaelic as a living language, in which case he would have nothing to do with us. But if we wished to study Gaelic as a dead language on a par with Latin and classical Greek, he would help us. Recognising the scholarly prejudice we were up against, Graham, Campbell and I did not disclose our " sentimental " leanings towards Gaelic as a spoken language, and so our class was established, attended that year by about a dozen undergraduates.

My father's comments on the professor's attitude were sharp. He wrote to me :

" Our worst enemies are our own kin in the east (of Scotland). They accepted the domination of the Saxon. Got the superiority complex in so doing, and no one looks on the west-coaster now so disdainfully as the east-coaster who has lost, or almost lost, his Gaelic heritage — and having come to that stage of transition, he never tires of shouting that Gaelic is dead and he does it with venom. A pure case of the fox that lost its tail. But for all that, Fraser is a valuable man to know and be influenced by, so far as his system of study is concerned. He would need to be born again, and that for preference in either Uist or Lewis. East is east and west is west, even in our own Gaeldom ".

My father added charitably : " . . . but he is a scholar without question and knows everything knowable about Gaelic literature ".

I could forgive Professor Fraser for taking an impersonal scholar's view of Gaelic, but not for castigating, in my hearing, the Rev.

---

* Now Duke of Montrose.
† Norman Macleod, 1783-1862. Moderator of the General Assembly of the Church of Scotland, 1836. *Caraid nan Gaidheal* consists partly of dialogues which first appeared in various Gaelic periodicals. According to the commentator Magnus Maclean, writing at the turn of the century, this work was " the greatest monument of Highland Gaelic original prose we have ".

Kenneth Macleod's* translations from Gaelic folksong lore as
" the bleatings of a sheep ". Kenneth Macleod educated the whole
world in Gaelic tradition, music and folklore. That year Fraser
had one student studying old Irish texts.

---

* Kenneth Macleod, 1872-1955. Minister on the islands of Colonsay and
Gigha. Folklorist. " A distinguished Gaelic scholar, Dr. Macleod was the
collector, the translator, and in a discreet measure even the composer of
The Songs of the Hebrides that were arranged and published by Mrs.
Kennedy-Fraser ". — *Glasgow Herald* obituary.

7

FEET, SCOTLAND, FEET!

"You did me proud", John Bannerman's father wrote to his son after a rugged International rugby match between Scotland and England. "Of course I am but natural in that, but even the *Bulletin* has ' Bannerman the Hero . . . ' "

For almost the entire 'twenties Bannerman was every Scots boy's hero on the rugby field, a stocky, bustling second-row forward who played hard for every second of the eighty minutes, a masterly controller of the ball who led those great forward rushes which typifield Scottish rugby between the wars.

His first love had been shinty. He mentions the games he saw at Shawlands Park, and others who were there recall the little boy who used to dash up and down the touchline shouting encouragement in Gaelic to the Glasgow Cowal team, until he became almost the team mascot and they were disappointed if he did not appear. Then he played soccer for Shawlands Academy, where he must have learned the dribbling techniques which made him outstanding on the rugby field. He captained Glasgow High School in 1919-20 when they were Western school rugby champions, having played 16 games, won 15, lost one, and drawn nil. Points for, 308; points against, 9.

Later he naturally played for Glasgow High School F.P. Between the High School and Glasgow Academicals there has always been fierce rivalry, and Bannerman could never resist a joke against his old enemies. Sometimes he claimed to be an honorary Academical because he played in the Glasgow inter-city team which included 12 Academicals and only two High School men — James Ireland and himself. One of his dearest rugby occasions came long after his playing days had ended, when he was invited as guest of honour to the dinner the Academicals held to celebrate the centenary of their club in 1966.

John Bannerman at the wheel of a tractor in 1931 when he was farm manager to the Duke of Montrose.

King George V meets the Scottish team before the 1922 international against England at Twickenham. Bannerman (second left) gained 37 consecutive caps playing for his country—a record which stood until 1962.

Father and son at the Dundee Mod in 1937. John R. Bannerman became president of An Comunn Gaidhealach the following year. John M. Bannerman was president in 1951.

John and Ray on the steps of Dornoch Cathedral after their wedding in 1931.

Campaigning with Ray before the Paisley by-election in 1961 in which Bannerman was narrowly defeated.

Scottish Television's fireside ceilidh team: John Bannerman, Fergie MacDonald, Evelyn Campbell and Alasdair Gillies.

Scottish Television picture.

It was as though they had searched for their greatest politico-football enemy and had found me! There were about 450 Academicals present in the school hall and I took great delight in telling them that the odds were just about right. But it was with complete sincerity that I had written to my former International colleague Herbert Waddell — a fitting president for their centenary year — accepting the invitation with these words : " No invitation could give me greater pleasure and no honour could be more acceptable ". That, however, did not prevent me from assuring them that for the next hundred years High School would continue to knock hell out of them on both sides of the fence which separates our grounds at Old Anniesland.

In my days as captain of School, J. B. " Jobby " White captained the Academy. Off the field, a kindlier fellow than " Jobby " would be difficult to find, but on the field he was a fierce leader and robust — to say the least — in his play. One bleak afternoon at Old Anniesland we were playing Academy before a big crowd. I lay at the bottom of a scrambling loose maul — face upwards, which wasn't very wise, but then I couldn't turn over. In those days the leather studs in our boots were held in place by little nails, and the leather wore more quickly than the nails. These scraped to and fro across my chest, and if I didn't recognise the boots, I did glimpse Jobby's legs inside them. When I got up I hissed at Jobby that " I would get him ".

Later in the game Jobby jumped and got the ball at a line-out. I was right behind him and I jumped on him, putting his head in a lock and at the same time " helping " him to retain the ball, which made my continuing attack legal. I exerted considerable pressure — and was mortified to find, after I let go, that a muscle in his neck and shoulder was sufficiently badly torn to force him to leave the field. I was full of remorse, having had no intention of making other than reasonable repayment for the scores on my chest. When the game finished and we were trooping from the field Jobby's father, Dr. John White, a great Scottish churchman and a Moderator of the General Assembly of the Church of Scotland, stopped me. I started to apologise, but Dr. White said, " Never mind, John, he got what was coming to him ".

A few years later I got more than I bargained for when I tried the same tactic in an International. It was in Colombe stadium in Paris; as usual in those days, Scotland were beating France. I am sorry to say I did the same thing to a Frenchman in a line-out as I had done to Jobby, but this time with dire effect to myself.

He was a black-faced, beetle-browed strongman from the south of France. Remembering Jobby, I didn't crush too hard, but I need not have worried. My arm being round his neck and conveniently near his mouth, he sank his strong teeth into my forearm. " Why don't you bark before you bite ", was my anguished retort, according to Ludi Stuart, with whom I shoved in the second row of the scrum for years for High School and Scotland. Mind you, Ludi had a lively imagination.

Another great School man, J. C. H. Ireland, was hooker for High School F.P. In those days there was often quite a duel between hookers. Jimmy was a good one, which meant that his opposite number had to look out. Playing Daniel Stewart's College at Old Anniesland on one occasion, Jimmy and the opposing hooker had been gently kicking one another when the incensed Stewart's man took the opportunity of loosing a blow at Jimmy when the front line were raising their heads preparatory to breaking up. Rather unintelligently, I continued to shove blindly from my position on the left of the second row, and my face came through to the place where Jimmy's had been. I received a most unexpected clout on the jaw, and naturally I clouted back. By this time Jimmy was some feet away and looking blandly innocent. The referee ran up to me and gave me a dressing down for ungentlemanly conduct. " Repeat that and you're off the field ", he growled. Speechless with indignation, I looked to my loyal comrades, including Jimmy, for vindication of my innocence. All they did was to increase my chagrin by laughing gleefully.

At Oxford it was inevitable that I should find myself shoving for Balliol in a Conservative scrum alongside Geordie Hamilton, Earl of Selkirk, and David Gordon of Haddo, now the Marquis of Aberdeen.

Next door in Bloody Trinity was Niall MacPherson, now Lord Drumalbyn, whose brother Phil was one of the brainiest centre three-quarters ever to play for Scotland. Niall and myself were members of the Oxford side that lost narrowly to Cambridge in 1928. Niall has since won at politics as a National Liberal, i.e. a Tory, while I kept on losing as a plain Liberal.

I consider the Varsity game, unlike most others I have played in, to be not so much a game as a war of attrition. I trained harder and talked tactics more for this game than for any International. The late A. B. Rodger, beloved Dean of Balliol, used to tell the story of how he asked me what special training I did for the Varsity game and how I was reputed to have replied, " Oh nothing much. Just changed over from Gold Flake to State Express ". The story, I fear, is apocryphal.

A story that can be vouched for, however, is the occasion on which Bannerman turned several of the Oxford side into temporary teetotallers. Before the Varsity match the team would finish their training at a resort on the coast, and on the way there hampers full of provisions would be handed in for consumption on the train. Normally there would be a large number of beer bottles in the order. Bannerman, much to the surprise of the purveyor, had pints of milk substituted for the pints of ale.

Always anxious for my welfare, my father sent me this advice in a letter written on board the Clyde steamer Lucy Ashton at Clynder on the eve of an International! " Just a wee word of cheer before you start for the scene of battle. Why should you worry? It is a game and let it be a strenuous one, keeping all your wits and good humour and enjoyment at their best till the whistle blows no side. Feed lightly on Friday evening and get into bed as early as you can. Read with all the reposeful interest usual to you and lie long in the morning. Tell them not to bring breakfast till you ring for it and see that your inside is in good order ". Sound advice. He also wrote drily after I was hurt in a game in 1929 : " I thought it was your knee you had strained, but as you proposed to go to a dance when I saw you I was of the opinion that there couldn't be much wrong with you. I knew for all that, that you would go to the same dance though it was only to dance on one foot . . . "

At Oxford in my time was Peter Howard, later to become of world influence as successor to Buchman as leader of the Moral Rearmament movement. I knew him well as a splendid rugby forward — although one of his legs below the knee was no thicker than my wrist. He used to roll bandages round it until it seemed to be of normal thickness under the stocking. I prevented him from getting his Blue that year as I felt it was too risky to play a man whose leg might break in two if kicked hard. Once my influence was removed he finally got his Blue and later played for and captained England. After a game at Murrayfield he remarked laughingly to me, " Thank heaven you left Oxford when you did, John, otherwise I would have had neither Blue nor International cap ". Anyone who knew Peter, whether an adherent of M.R.A.

or not, saw in him a wholly admirable man. I can pay him no
greater tribute than to say he had the same qualities of honesty
and dedication as Eric Liddell, with whom I also played, and that
he later inspired by writing, spoken word and example, millions
of people throughout the world to seek unselfishness rather than
selfishness, love rather than hate.

Also in the 1927-8 Oxford side in which I played was J. P. W.
Mallalieu.* If Curly Mallalieu does his job as well as when we
were being hammered on our line by Cambridge, the country and
its economy should be quite safe.

By the time I was at Oxford my International career was nearing
its end. One of the earliest Internationals to stand out in my mind
was the game at Dublin in 1921, when I woke up in my bedroom
in the Shelbourne Hotel to see khaki figures with rifles climbing
over the roofs of buildings across the street. A raid was on. The
warlike atmosphere engendered by " the Troubles " continued at
the Lansdowne Road ground, for we ran on to the field through
a detachment of soldiers lined up along the touchline with fixed
bayonets. They remained there, facing the crowd, during the whole
game, but the banter off and on the field was light-hearted.
Whoever scored against Ireland, they said, was bound to be shot.
But we won that game and managed to escape execution.

But those were bitter days and there was little to laugh at in
Dublin. There was a 9 p.m. curfew and we had to travel in
armoured cars to a dance in the Castle. However, our dinner was
the usual hilarious — and destructive — affair, with Phil the
Fluter's Ball sung on the table-top amidst the dishes. Only in
Ireland and from an Irishman could this cheerful postscript be
added to that era of the Black and Tans. This Irishman was
enormous and insisted on haranguing us from the table-top. " I
only play International football, and would you like to know why? "
he roared at one point in his rich brogue, " Because the rest of
me club's in jail! " My memory is that he made this disconcerting
pronouncement quite cheerfully. Whether his satisfaction stemmed
from the fact that he himself had escaped jail or that he was free
from the chore of playing club football, only an Irishman like
himself could have told.

It was significant that our International dinner was always held

---

* Labour M.P. for Huddersfield East. Minister of Trade in the Harold
Wilson government.

not in a hotel but in rooms entered from the street by a dark, narrow passage. The rooms were bare of ornament and could take no harm no matter how boisterous the dinner became. One of the characters in these dinners was the famous " Jammy " Clinch, who became a successful and respected doctor in South Wales and has now retired to live in Dublin. At that time he was a powerful forward who always wore what looked like a Roman circlet round his head. His slow, deep-voiced witticisms in heavy Irish brogue were cherished. When a fellow Irishman dropped a pass from him, Jammy rounded on him, " Ach, ye wad think I was handing ye an illegitimate child ". The main course dishes were still before us at one of the Irish dinners when Jammy proceeded to one end of the 30-foot section table and in his sepulchral voice announced that he would now demonstrate how to remove the great white tablecloth, leaving the dishes exactly where they were. Bunching the ends of the cloth in his great fists, he pulled backwards, and disappeared in an avalanche of white cloth and dishes. Irish oaths filled the air — but somehow order was restored and the dinner was calmly continued.

Great days and great fellows! No doubt it is my Liberal bias, but I wish I knew less of the political history that culminated in the 1916 Rebellion and the Black and Tan era. Bitterness and bloodshed could have been avoided by Home Rule and the proud partnership of Great Britain and Ireland might still have been intact. As it is, rugby is the only game that transcends the political differences between Eire and Northern Ireland.

When my International career began in 1921, the immediate post-war sides had been made up of old salts and old soldiers like Jock Wemyss, Finlay Kennedy, Charlie Usher and A. T. Sloan — men who would have played scores of Internationals had they not been fighting the greater battles of the First War. Wemyss to me is the symbol of the Scottish forward, a man who in his play, his written commentaries on the game,* and in his patriotic enthusiasm epitomises all that is best in the spirit of rugby. His marking of a big Frenchman nicknamed the Mayor of Toulouse in a game at Colombe is legendary. Both men were minus one eye — but Jock soon showed himself more than a match for the Mayor.

In 1921 I was the youngest member of the Scottish team to

* Jock Wemyss was for many years rugby correspondent of the *Scottish Daily Express*.

play in Wales. I was sitting in the pavilion before we went on the field when I first heard 50,000 singing *Land of my Fathers,* and I could have done with my father being with me! As a brother Celt I can appreciate the effect their music has on the game, and I thrill to the patriotic fervour of the song, sung as only Welsh voices can sing it. It must be the winning factor for many a Welsh side. At Murrayfield we do not sing *Scots Wha Hae,* or even *Scotland the Brave.* In any case many of us would not know the words. And perhaps the English would not approve.

But it was the enthusiasm of the Welsh crowd that lost Wales the game that day. Having broken through the barriers, they sat quietly enough on the touchline till the Welsh side pressed us in the corner, when those at the far end would run on to the field to get a better view of what was happening. The referee would immediately stop the game and mounted police would come on to clear the pitch. Our lighter Scottish pack could then get a much needed breather, for we were being battered by the mighty Welsh forwards, off whom we bounced as off a wall. It seemed to me that the Welsh forwards then were either policemen or miners — the one kind took you by the scruff of the neck and became angry if you didn't come along quietly, and the other attacked you as though you were the coal face and he was on piecework. But we won.

In 1923 there was also a break-in by the crowd, this time at Cardiff Arms Park, and we were again victorious, in the main due to hard, bustling forwards and to A. L. Gracie, whose try still ranks as a classic in rugby football. Describing the game, the *Times* said : " Then followed the great forward battle in which, strange to relate on a Welsh ground, the Scotsmen finally rushed and counter-rushed the Welshmen very nearly to a standstill ". It was a good forward line : J. C. R. " Buckie " Buchanan, Stewarts; L. M. " Ludi " Stuart Glasgow High School — the youngest forward, who had a touchdown; D. S. Doug Davies, Hawick; J. R. " Jock " Lawrie, Melrose; D. M. " Tubby " Bertram, Watsonians; D. (for David) S. Kerr, Heriots; A. K. " Jumbo " Stevenson, Glasgow Academicals; and myself.

We owed our victory also to Eric Liddell, playing on the wing in that game. Liddell was a quiet, unassuming Scot, a great Olympic athlete and rugby player who gained worldwide respect for his simple action of refusing to run on a Sunday at the 1924 Olympic Games in Paris — an action which lost him the chance of winning an Olympic gold medal in the 100 metres, the race for which he had trained. Later in the week he won a gold medal for the 400 metres, which was not his chosen distance. Liddell went to China as a missionary and died in a Japanese war camp. He was a humble man with a fighting faith.

In 1925 came my proudest moment in rugby, at the end of the game in which we opened Murrayfield stadium. W. W. Wakefield, later Lord Wakefield, led the fast, heavy pack of English forwards. He himself was hard, efficient, a great scrummager and dangerous in the open — a close-cropped, bullet-headed yeoman of England. Put Cromwell helmets on Wakefield and his colleagues and you would have had a modern troop of Ironsides. Even the white jersey of England with its red rose was somehow a symbol of confident superiority compared to the dark blue of Scotland, a sombre background for the thistle.

This was no ordinary International. Was our great Murrayfield stadium with its emerald turf to be hanselled by defeat — and by the Auld Enemy? Perish the thought! But as the game progressed, Wakefield and his men seemed more than usually confident and determined to make it another Flodden. In the end the tide was turned for us by two Glasgow Academicals, Nelson with a clever try and Waddell with a magnificent drop goal which gained the vital points. When the whistle blew leaving Scotland victorious by 19 points to 15, I was astounded to see a number of English forwards flop to the ground where they stood, utterly exhausted and beaten. Yeomen of England they might be, a great race dominant in the world, but in dour old Scotland on this occasion at least they were beaten to their knees. More accurately, to their backsides.

One personal incident in that game which was Scotland's first victory over England since 1912 and won us the Triple Crown, remains clear in my memory. We were pressing and mauling on the English 25 near the right touchline. By some strange chance I found myself clutching the ball to the small of my back with my left arm. I didn't know how it had got there, and no one else seemed to know where it was. Had I nonchalantly strolled towards the English line nobody would have taken any notice of me and I might have scored. As it was, I galloped along the right touchline and reached within three or four yards of the English line. Then a thunderbolt hit me, lifting me yards over the touchline. It was "Wakers", the only man who had tumbled to the situation. I couldn't hand him off, for my left arm was still crooked over the ball in the small of my back. I don't remember ever being hit so hard or travelling so far as a result of a tackle.

Harry Simpson was the Secretary of the Scottish Rugby Union for so long during this period that he might have been built in. He was an Edinburgh lawyer, a Writer to the Signet, with a dry humour, who was seldom known to make a complimentary remark to anyone's face, and yet he was greatly loved. Among his many duties was the responsibility of making sure that International and trial sides were ready for the field at the advertised times, a task in which he seemed to find greatest difficulty with the Glasgow High School men, Ludi Stuart, Jimmy Ireland and myself. He used to say we caused him more trouble than all the rest put together. Harry's disgruntlement was brought to an almost apoplectic climax on the day of a final trial in Edinburgh. I had received my usual perforated postcard and had returned the half to say I should be free and fit to play. I did not read it very carefully or take note of the time the game was due to start, and travelled to Edinburgh by the train which took us to our ordinary Saturday club games there. It reached Waverley station after two o'clock and I arrived to find that the trial had been started for some minutes. I changed in frantic haste and was running from the back of the pavilion when Harry met me. " That's finished you, Bannerman ", said Harry (who usually called me John), " you needn't bother to go on ". I went back, changed again and sat forlornly in the almost deserted stand. Shortly after the half-time whistle blew, Harry came bouncing up to me, having been instructed by the selectors to tell me to go on. When he saw that I was in my ordinary clothes he nearly exploded. " My God, Bannerman, you're going to be late for the second half too ! " As indeed I was, by about three minutes. I knew then that I would have to play hard to keep my place, but the dice were loaded in my favour as I was fresh and the other fellows exhausted by a gruelling first half. I was again selected for the International team, in spite of Harry's remark : " If I had anything to do with the selection of the side, Bannerman, you'd never get another cap ". This was spoken in his usual vein, and I took it as a compliment.

Bannerman got his caps so regularly that team-mates jokingly accused him of bribing the selectors with State Express, his favourite brand of cigarette. He was the natural choice for Scotland from his first appearance against France in 1921 to his last against England in 1929, and his International career

could clearly have continued but for his decision to take up
a scholarship in America. Press reports of his last game at
Murrayfield were ecstatic. Probably he would have been
capped again on his return from America, but word got about
— erroneously — in high places that he did not wish to be
considered for selection, and in fact he played little rugby
afterwards.

His record of 37 consecutive Scottish caps was not surpassed
until 1962, and it was achieved at a time when fewer Internationals were played than today. In 25 of these 37 games
he was on the winning side, and in the golden years 1925-27
Scotland won ten out of twelve games.

Bannerman was always superbly fit, even though he appeared
to undertake little formal training. Others might spend
summer nights keeping in trim by running round Ibrox,
Queen's Park, or whatever football pitch was nearest to their
homes, but not Bannerman. " He did his own training in his
own way ", James Ireland recalls. " He used to arrive for the
rugby season, probably having walked mile after mile in Skye.
He'd be soft, but as fit as a fiddle ".

Once in the ruck he never let up, like a dog worrying a bone,
He'd play hard till the whistle blew and his legs were shaky,
and he never seems to have had a bad game.

He took plenty of knocks. In one club game he lost teeth and
told no one. His remedy for legs torn and bleeding under the
mud was to scrub them with a brush. And a less stoical man
might have called off from the first International he played
against France, for just before the game he emptied a cup of
scalding tea over his stomach.

By today's standards of fast-moving, heavy forwards, Bannerman was slow and light (he was not much more than 13 stone).
But his temperament was ideal and his physique perfect;
well-knit, with sturdy legs and well-muscled shoulders. His
footwork was unequalled. In one club game he is said to have
dribbled the awkward ball from one end of the pitch to the
other.

These were the great days of cross-dribbling, now vanished
from the game, when rugby forwards would spread across the
field a yard or two apart and sweep onwards, passing the ball
between them with their feet. It was a difficulty skill to acquire,
and Bannerman and his fellow High School men spent hours
in the scrum room or dribbling down the length of the fence

at Old Anniesland practising technique. Good cross-dribbling made the pack a mighty offensive machine and Bannerman, as leader of the Scottish pack, made full use of it. Even when Scotland had the Oxford three-quarter line on the field he made sure that when the forwards got the ball they held on to it more often than not, a tactic for which he was criticised. The criticism had no effect.

Bannerman enjoyed the exuberant atmosphere surrounding International rugby trips almost as much as the game itself. Before a Welsh game, when he should probably have been early to bed in his Cardiff hotel, he insisted on declaiming a play he was rehearsing to his room-mate, Herbert Waddell. The play was in Gaelic, of which Waddell understood not a word. In Paris afterwards he aroused the admiration of the French in his kilt. And it was said that every good player in England, Ireland, Wales and France had heard the *Eriskay Love Lilt* sung as a duet by Johnny Bannerman and Jimmy Ireland.

His enthusiasm for the game was infectious. He spoke little during a match, but always had a grin on his face. One of the few times his temper was roused on the field was when the Welsh forwards at Cardiff in 1923 kicked Gracie as he lay on the ball. Bannerman rolled up his sleeves, set his face, and waded into the tussle with furious energy.

He was a natural attacking player who played to win, not to avoid defeat. When, later in life, he harked back to attacking forward play he was thinking of the spirit of his own playing days when it was a sin to kick for touch and it required no law to keep the ball in play. Not surprisingly, he abominated the tactics of negative, defensive football which prevailed for so long after the last war.

The Scottish Rugby Union is regarded as a conservative body by the public, which is an adjective I am opposed to in another context. But as applied to the Union it emphasises the splendid leadership of such men as Aikman Smith, president of the S.R.U. in the 'twenties, and a host of others who have controlled the destiny of rugby in Scotland. The game is for the player, is the maxim. The S.R.U. has always judged all questions in that light, with splendid effect in preserving the amateur status of the game in Scotland.

I have always been of the opinion that rugby was a game to be played and not talked about, and I hope I am not transgressing the amateur laws of the Scottish Rugby Union in giving my reminiscences. For if there is one thing I am proud of in Scottish rugby it is the true amateur status of the game. Rugby is a game of worth, to be enjoyed by the player for its skills and its sciences and for the lessons it teaches.

Thanks largely to Bannerman's opposition, Scotland was the last home team to number its players. "The game is for the player" — and therefore anything which might introduce personality into the game and make it a spectator sport was to be frowned on.

Some of the merit rugby contains for the player has been taken from the game during my lifetime in order to provide a greater "spectacle". Any change of law to protect the player from serious injury is justifiable, but to pass legislation designed to limit the skill and speed of the wing forward so that the ball may pass freely to the three-quarters is to limit the science of scrummaging and to reduce the forward to mere heeling machines. We had wing forwards in my day playing in the 3-2-3 scrum formation, and we needed no law to protect our stand-off from them. If wing forwards troubled us we might hold the ball, putting them off-side. Or we might wheel the scrum, beating the scrum half and then the wing forward with a cross pass before driving forward. When we had the wing forward in two minds about breaking too quickly from a set scrum — *then* we would shoot the ball back through the channel formed by our feet, out and away from the scrum half to stand-off to centre, and finally to the wing. Then might we see Ian Smith making glorious dives to score just inside the far corner flag. That was a spectacle for you! Even with all the new laws, how often do you see this happen today? Perhaps my viewpoint is biassed, but it stems from experience. Deprive the forward of his traditional science and technique of scrummaging, and the authority to lay down the pattern of the game, and you deprive rugby of its original merit, the quality which first made it a game to conjure with when there were no backs at all.

Forward play science saves forwards from running uselessly about the field trying to retrieve a ball that should not have been blindly and unintelligently backed in the first place. In the old days, if the three-quarters fumbled the ball two or three times running when we put it back to them, we would get fed up with

going back to retrieve it at considerable expenditure of energy.
Coldly and calmly we would decide, enough of that! We would
then hold the ball, wheel with it and take it forward — anywhere
but back to the backs! — until we were in a position to give it
to them on a plate. One or two of the defence would be down
on the ball and our backs would have the advantage of at least
one man over. Then they could hardly fail to do something
constructive with the ball.

Changes in the law, introduced without the player's consent and
not designed for his benefit, have failed lamentably to make the
game more spectacular. There is now the ludicrous business of the
line-out which looks more like the chorus of the Bolshoi Ballet —
arms outstretched not to catch the ball but to pat it back. One
expects a forward to say " Excuse me " if he has inadvertently
pushed his opposite number. Not even an apology would mitigate
the crime, for the referee blows a shocked whistle immediately.

Forwards at the line-out required no referee's whistle to protect
them in the old days. I remember a game in Wales when two or
more forwards bent on obstruction gathered round their colleague
to whom the ball was to be thrown. How did we combat these
" disgraceful " tactics? Why, one of us, standing a yard away from
the line-out, made a flying leap inwards when the ball was thrown
in. The aim was not to get the ball. The two obstructing forwards
were spreadeagled and someone else slipped into the space created
and dealt with the Welshman who thought he was safe to catch
the ball. Exhilarating times these were when brain as well as brawn
counted, and tactics were constantly changed.

There is a mistaken notion that open, constructive play can be
got by shouting loudly to have the ball back. This develops a
basketball passing type of rugby which ends in frustration, especially
for the centre three-quarter. It makes a mockery of rugby's worth
as a game for the player and is a killer for forwards. Today the
slow, heavy, hard-working forward is being legislated out of the
game because spectacle-loving spectators whose knowledge of the
science of forward play may be nil. I will generously admit that
the fleet-footed among us are due a game. Let there be half backs
and three-quarters — but let them be the servants, not the masters,
of the forwards.

With the present monopoly of the 3-4-1 scrum formation nothing
much *can* be done but back the ball. In my opinion we should at
least vary the formation between 3-4-1 and 3-2-3, depending on
what the forwards plan to do with the ball. When I became vice-

president of the Scottish Rugby Union in 1953* Scotland had the inglorious record of no win in 17 consecutive games. Having been beaten 44-nil at Murrayfield by the South Africans in 1951 we threw over our traditional Scottish forward play which used the feet as well as the hands and decided to follow the great African " masters ", adopt the 3-4-1 scrum formation and plan an " open " game. The Scots forwards became a heeling machine. Gone were the cries of " Feet, Scotland, feet! " and defeat, sometimes ignominious, was our portion for the succeeding years.

You throw your traditions overboard at your own peril. Backed by Herbert Waddell and the Union committee, I proposed a return to the 3-2-3 scrum formation, at least as a variant to 3-4-1. Eight hard-working, powerful forwards were picked — not brilliant outside men, but men who by close scrummaging tactics, wheeling and the use of the foot rush, forced some of the most fancied, fleet-footed teams from other countries to try to combat our own Scottish forward tactics. In doing so they became less fleet-footed. We actually started to win and were again a team to be reckoned with in the Triple Crown and Calcutta Cup games. My satisfaction was not that we occasionally won, but that we were no longer to be patted on the back patronisingly by England — or even France! — with the remark, " If there is anyone we'd like to beat us it's Scotland ". They would then proceed to the field to knock us for six. Fierce, traditional Scottish forward play, in the phrase used by Jock Wemyss to me, " stopped that nonsense ".

I hope that Scotland will never forget the lesson we learned in rugby and will seek to apply it in all Scottish matters. Take what is good from other countries, test it and use it, but never allow the natural, traditional Scottish methods and outlook to be submerged. " Adopt, adapt and improve " is the motto of the Round Table, and we could well use it as our national motto against the relegation of Scottish traditions in any sphere into second place, or oblivion.

Scotland has a unique position in the respect and affection of the peoples of the world with whom she has had any contact. She retains this regard in spite of the standardising influence and dictation of centralised government in London. It says much for the tenacity and distinctive qualities of the Scot and for the worth of his institutions that we still survive the greatest takeover bid in

* Bannerman was president of the S.R.U. for the year 1954-55.

history — the submergence and the absorption of the Scottish Parliament by its English counterpart in 1707.

This seems a far cry from the subject of Scottish rugby. But it is relevant in that it shows that we do not necessarily gain by adopting alien ideas. To allow our traditional methods of play to be submerged by the total acceptance of other countries' methods is to ignore two facts : the climate of Scotland and the soft, muddy pitches on which we play, and the dour, tough quality of Scotsmen attuned to solid work rather than to the more spectacular methods of open play appropriate to drier countries. It should be more widely appreciated that it was no accident we won Bannockburn in such style — not by copying England's flamboyant cavalry charges, but by the phlegmatic, prosaic method of digging holes in the boggy ground into which the pride of English chivalry obligingly fell.

8

WITH ARCHIBALD ACROSS AMERICA

OF my three years' scholarship, two were to be spent at Oxford and the third in America. So in autumn of 1929 I said goodbye to rugby and its records and made for Washington D.C. to work in the Bureau of Economics for three months. I then matriculated at Cornell University, Ithaca, for six months' research on farm machinery. I learned that the Americans, by aid of card-punching machines — pointers to the computer age just round the corner — were prepared to correlate any factor, even the colour of the tractor driver's eyes, to the yield per acre of the barley he was cutting.

Even in the dire depression of the 'thirties the Americans impressed me, cut-throat as they might be in industry and business, as open and generous in social life. There was a strange paradox of ruthless super-efficiency and energy in making dollars and a full-handed generosity when it came to spending them.

Prohibition laws were openly flouted in speakeasies that were as numerous and blatant in New York streets as our pubs in Paisley Road West, Glasgow. At the socialite dances, instead of cocktail bars, cases of whisky lay around in the corridors with supplies of paper cups. Result: disorderly drinking, and drunks everywhere. A real lesson that morals and behaviour can be worsened by legislation which does not have the widespread consent or approval of the people.

I arrived by the S.S. Caledonia in New York, where my kilt evening rig-out had its first and last airing in the U.S.A. I went to the Waldorf-Astoria dressed in kilt and doublet for a dinner-dance and cabaret — an exclusive affair to which some American friends had invited me. As I was heading for the vestibule a white-gloved, brocaded commissionaire shouted at me in taxi-hailing tone: " Not that way, bud — cabaret artistes this way! "

It was obvious to me, seeing most of the magnificent university campuses in America, that she was laying the foundation of

universal higher grade education far ahead of this country. She
might not reach the peaks of intellectual achievement attained by
a small number in this country. But at university level, which we
tend to decry as high school standard, every kind of study was
available to millions. There were opportunities in post-school
education which, in England at least, we are only now beginning
to provide, more than thirty years later.

As a Scot I received a warmer welcome than is reputedly
accorded the "Limey" or Englishman. Maybe this attitude stems
from the American Revolution and resentment towards the Englishman as one of a ruling race. Maybe there is sympathy for the
Scot as one of a race which is subject, at least politically, to the
English. Scottish pedigree is stressed and nurtured by Americans
even when generations removed from Scotland.

I visited a hospitable family whose name was Calhoun. They
counted themselves an American branch of the Colquhoun clan.
Their house in the country was the American conception of what
a Scottish chief's keep should be. I entered through a baronial
lodge and circled up a long drive to a small replica of a Scottish
castle, to which entry was obtained over a drawbridge spanning a
moat. There was even a portcullis over the door. Inside was
centrally-heated luxury, with thistle emblems everywhere on
carpets, carved on doors and on the ornate balustrades of the
main stairs, which rose from the centre of the great hall. Here was
luxurious, functional comfort allied to an almost painfully sentimental worship of tartan Scotland. The rugs were tartan; so were
the great curtains on the hall windows.

Money had made this extravaganza possible. It was an
exaggerated symbol of the warm corner Scotland and its heroic
clan history has in the heart of many Americans with even remote
claims to Scottish kinship.

For a Scotsman, the economic depression had its points. I was
able to buy a 31 h.p. Buick tourer for 75 dollars. I then picked up
a fellow countryman from Oxford, J. J. MacGregor, at Winsconsin
University, and together we visited most of the agricultural state
colleges in the middle and western states. Finally we reached Los
Angeles and found ourselves, through the influence of Scots friends,
members of a select beach club where we rubbed shoulders with
Charlie Chaplin and looked in awe at the gold door knockers on
the holiday house of some film star.

Mac and I then proceeded up the Great Pacific Highway to
San Francisco. There was a "gas" war in full swing during our

Lord Bannerman on the day of his introduction to the House of Lords (December 6th, 1967). He told the Lords: " As soon as the equivalent House is set up in Edinburgh I shall gladly take the shorter journey."

MR. JOHN M. BANNERMAN.

President of the Scottish Rugby Union in 1954 — champion of 3-2-3 scrummaging and aggressive forward play.

Bannerman in the grounds of the Old Manse overlooking Loch Lomond.

Scottish Daily Express picture.

Lord and Lady Bannerman . . . their last picture together.

The family at the Old Manse. Left to right: John, Elizabeth, John M.
Bannerman, Janet, Ray, and Calum.

trip, and as we moved west and north the petrol became cheaper and cheaper until we arrived at Portland, Oregon, where we got it for nothing if we bought oil. As the Buick burned oil like petrol, we filled up with petrol continually at next-to-nothing in cost. A real Scotsman's trip, for after touring back through Canada and over the Rockies, I sold the Buick for 25 dollars.

The trip had a pioneering character for the two young men often slept rough, and the car — a 1923 model which they christened Archibald — could be as stubborn as a mule. Bowling along the long, straight roads of the Mid-West (which were sprayed with oil to keep down the dust) or limping into town with steam jetting from Archibald's radiator, they logged more than 6,000 miles altogether, and Bannerman went on to cover considerably more on his own.

Every morning on the road, Archibald would be loaded with their brown canvas lean-to tent, an extra spare tyre, two camp beds, four blankets, a collection of tin cooking pans and cutlery stowed for convenience in a bucket, two large trunks and a couple of suitcases. Topping the lot and sticking up in the back seat would be their golf clubs, which they wielded with mixed effect at various stops on the way.

The first breakdown came after a week on the road. At the end of 284 miles, the lengthiest daily total so far, the Buick puttered to a stop with a petrol leak which had emptied the tank. There was also a flat tyre, but that was secondary. MacGregor suggested that they should walk on to the nearest filling station and bring back enough petrol to get them to town, but Bannerman insisted they were miles from anywhere, and they bedded down uncomfortably for the night. "Always dogmatic in his opinions", MacGregor reflected ruefully the next morning when they found a pump half-a-mile along the road.

During the latter part of the journey they had continual trouble with the battery. "Where's the blooming old handle?" cried Bannerman one morning in vexation when the self-starter would not work. It was no good; the starting handle had been mislaid and they had to wait for a tow from their camping site. Hopes were raised by the arrival of a tourist in an old Ford which he had stripped to the chassis (his baggage was wrapped in a blanket and strapped to the petrol tank). But the Ford proved too light for the job, and, anyway, neither party had a rope. Finally they were hauled up the grassy bank and on to the highway by the driver of a car whose wife claimed Scots ancestry.

Their first day north of the Canadian border ended with them being towed behind a broken-down nag and a light cart. In San Francisco, a reversing lorry burst the radiator and shattered a headlamp, and at an auto camp near Hollywood they nearly lost Archibald for good. They left the car parked on a slope while booking into the auto camp — a forerunner of today's motels — and returned to find it rolling down the hill at gathering speed. They sprinted after and managed to stop it before damage was done, the only mishap in the excitement being a carton of porridge oats which had been carried safely across the continent and now burst, spreading its contents over the rear seat.

This was a midsummer journey and for most of the time the sun shone. For the first few days they suffered from thunderstorms and the rain came through the roof of their tent in a fine spray. Later, in Bryce Canyon, they awoke early to find a heavy dew seeping through the canvas and dripping on their faces. It was a good excuse for some early morning fishing, which they performed using tent poles as rods. MacGregor caught a couple of good fish and Bannerman a handful of what he scornfully described as " baggy minnows ". They threw the lot in the pan and made a tasty breakfast.

In Oregon, Bannerman tried fishing of another sort, diving underwater in an attempt to salvage a fountain pen which the nearby storekeeper's son had lost in a deep river pool. When this failed, he took boyish pleasure in hanging head first from the end of a board — with MacGregor on the other end as a counter-weight — and scooping the pen from the river bed with a tin pan tied to a pole. He then insisted on scooping up a pair of sunglasses which could also be seen in the depths of the pool.

As the sun grew stronger they peeled off clothes, down to shorts in the case of Bannerman and white running strip for MacGregor. " Hi, where's your pants? " hollered a bystander. It was a bad move for Bannerman, who suffered so badly from mosquito bites on the legs that he had to get medical attention in Denver.

Bannerman, as always, was most at home in casual clothes. Approaching Los Angeles it was agreed that MacGregor should call at the bank rather than Bannerman, who at the time was sporting his purple-striped pyjama top in place of a shirt. And he was only parted from a favourite but well worn pair of blue plus-fours when the seat disintegrated. He had to make an embarrassed, crab-like entry into a small town store for replacements, which turned out to be linen plus-fours so pale they were almost white, patterned in a gaudy check.

Often they would drop into a picture house for amusement on the way, sometimes recognising movie stars they had seen in the flesh in Los Angeles. (MacGregor almost summoned up courage to introduce himself to the glamorous Dorothy Mackail as she walked along the Santa Monica beach at sunset dressed in an alluring white sweater and blue sailor-boy slacks, when he was deterred by Bannerman's withering growl, " Ach, *Mac* . . . ! ")

Plain eating suited Bannerman best; several times he quashed MacGregor's inclination to try exotic foods in places like the Japanese Tea Garden in San Francisco. His favourite drink was malted milk from the drug stores — an ice-cream and a large glass of milk was a common request, illustrated by outstretched hands and a broad smile.

The tour was a lot of fun. They yelled " Howdy " to startled bystanders as they whirled past in the Buick. They were always ready to raise their voices in song with their American hosts (and were asked kindly not to in a Chicago cafe). Bannerman strummed Gaelic airs on a piano in Salt Lake City, where they also danced on the " largest semi-open air dancing floor in America ".

But they did not forget the serious purpose of their visit to the States, taking the chance of visiting farms and colleges. They saw, for example, the world's largest herd of Guernsey cattle at a Californian dairy farm and they inspected a herd of pedigree Ayrshires in the Fraser River valley as they passed through British Columbia.

From British Columbia we motored on to Winnipeg and thence south to New York State. My impression of Canada in the early 'thirties was of a country gasping for capital investment. I liked the hardiness and kindliness of the Canadians, and their immense patriotism for Great Britain and their own country. We found no belligerent French feeling, perhaps because we did not go far enough east.

In Vancouver I borrowed dress clothes from the digs of the
absent Canadian Minister of Defence, the late Iain McKenzie, a
famous son of the Highlands of Scotland. This I did through the
good offices of the late Angus MacLeod, who shared McKenzie's
digs. Angus was the eldest son of Duncan MacLeod of Skeabost,
Isle of Skye, a great benefactor of his people and island. Angus
and I had been invited to attend a Governor's reception and dance
in Victoria Island. I was denied a very active part in the dance
because McKenzie's clothes, cut for his slim figure, stuck to me
like a tight glove.

Our method of transport to the reception was unusual; a tiny
aeroplane with a couple of water skids instead of wheels enabled
us to take off from the Fraser River at Vancouver and come down
in the harbour at Victoria.

One morning on my way through Canada, I was having breakfast in a cafeteria in Medicine Hat when a bearded, middle-aged
man climbed on to the stool next to me and asked for " the usual "
in what seemed a good Highland accent. I thought at first I might
be mistaken, but when a plate of steaming porridge was placed
before him my doubts vanished and I addressed him in Gaelic.
His face lit up, and I am sure the porridge took on a different
blas, taste. He was a second generation MacLean from Argyll, but
by his Gaelic and indeed his English he could have been born on
the croft by the island shore.

Canada is the better for the distinctive contribution to her
development made by Scottish Highlanders who, like this MacLean,
retain their love for their Highland traditions and language. Those
who would standardise everything should confine themselves to
the corn beef tin. They have little appreciation of the benefits they
would sacrifice on the altar of uniformity.

9

FACTOR TO THE DUKE

BANNERMAN came back from America to marry — and to find
a job. He toyed with the idea of going to the Far East as a
field officer for I.C.I., but in the end decided to stay where
he belonged, influenced partly, no doubt, by Ray Mundell,
the dark-haired farmer's daughter from Sutherland whom he
would shortly marry in Dornoch Cathedral. Besides, he was
greatly attracted by the offer of another post in the west of
Scotland. During his stay with Donald MacKelvie in Arran,
Bannerman had become acquainted with the Duke and
Duchess of Montrose, who spent each summer at Brodick
Castle, and one of his close friends at Oxford had been their
son, the Marquis of Graham. On his return to Scotland in
1930 Bannerman was offered the post of farm manager on
the Montrose Estates, which covered a large stretch of farm
and hill land to the south and east of Loch Lomond, and
though his father was opposed to what he considered a waste
of talent on crop husbandry and animal management, Bannerman accepted. It was not long before he was also appointed
factor. Bannerman moved from his temporary room in
Buchanan Castle to live with his bride in the picturesque
Old Manse at Balmaha, where they also took over the
adjoining farm.

The relationship between Bannerman and the Duke was
more that of friends than master and man. " What Gael but
would revere a family whose eldest son and heir took the
trouble and interest to write, speak and sing like a native
in the Gaelic language ", he wrote, and his loyalty was
unswerving.

The Duchess, formerly Lady Mary Hamilton, played the
violin and piano and used to accompany Bannerman when
he sang at social gatherings at Buchanan Castle or Brodick
(where the young man was once covered with confusion when

his kilt swept the tea things from the table, to fall in a crash
of china and silverware on the floor). There were lively ceilidhs
at both the castle and the Old Manse, and Bannerman
converted the Duke and Duchess into enthusiastic attenders
of the Mod. He also attempted to teach the Duchess Gaelic
by his usual method of refusing to conduct a conversation in
any other language. Family parties consisting of the Duke and
Duchess, their daughter Jean (now Lady Jean Fforde) and
the Bannermans regularly drove to the Murrayfield rugby
Internationals, and Lady Jean remembers her mother bringing
steaming plates of soup down to the frozen pond at Drymen
while the menfolk enjoyed a game of curling.

The Marquis of Graham was absent from these gatherings.
Unlike Bannerman, *Aonghas Mor* had taken a job abroad
with I.C.I. This took him to what was then Southern Rhodesia,
where he eventually settled and took to farming. He was
Minister of Agriculture in the Smith Government which
declared U.D.I., and later Minister of Defence.

Aonghas Mor invaded the veldt and carved a farm for himself
and his family from the wilderness, building farmhouse and
steading with his own hands. Now, having sold the farm he
pioneered at a well-deserved profit, the Duke (as he now is) farms
near Salisbury, sending hundreds of gallons of milk daily to that
town.

When Mr. Wilson was asked in 1966 in the House of Commons
what steps he would take to deprive the " rebellious " Duke of
Montrose of his seat in the House of Lords, the then Prime
Minister's reply was that there was no need to take a sledgehammer
to crack a nut, especially that kind of nut — at which there was
loud laughter. Mr. Wilson then said that anyone who had met
the Duke, as he had, would not treat him seriously. Yet but for
such " nuts " as Montrose, who commanded a destroyer at Crete
and throughout the Second World War, Mr. Wilson would not
have been in a position to exercise his wit. Had he, like Queen
Juliana of the Netherlands, been rescued by *Aonghas Mor's*
destroyer when the Germans overran Holland, he might have
refrained from being so harsh.

The Duchess, like her son, studied the Gaelic language but never
mastered the accent as well as he did. As Lady Mary Hamilton
she was rich and beautiful — and, besides, a fearless rider to
hounds and an excellent shot. But she proved her gentle qualities

as an indefatigable nurse and benefactor to the wounded men of two world wars. She was a woman of intensely practical character and no job, however difficult or menial, did she shrink from. As a farmer and gardener she knew as much as the grieve or the workman, and the nation is the richer today for the layout of Brodick Castle gardens and their outstanding specie rhododendrons, now the property of the National Trust.

James, 6th Duke of Montrose, although educated at Eton, was all his life a bulwark for Scotland against the dominance of English influences. He was a catholic and careful reader, and perhaps because of his deafness he took little account of passing fashion around him. That is not to say that he dwelt in the past, for there was nothing he liked better than to settle down in an armchair after dinner and with the help of his hearing aid discuss exhaustively the issues of the day with his family and friends.

Perhaps it was because both men were unconventional characters that Bannerman and the Duke took to each other. The Duke had spent his early life at sea, becoming a master mariner under sail (and later in life giving his memoirs the sailorlike title of *My Ditty Box*). The entry he wrote for *Who's Who* includes two remarkable claims: " Inventor and designer of the first naval aircraft carrying ship ", and " Obtained the first films ever taken of a total eclipse of the sun, R.A.S. Expedition, India, 1899 ". His deafness, caused by a gun being fired close to his ear when he was a child, was severe and he always carried a deaf aid which looked like a small attaché case. He remained very active until his death in January 1954 at the age of 75.

In 1902, owing to his interest and enthusiasm, the R.N.V.R. was created. He campaigned for better food and quarters for the crews of British ships and condemned the dietary for young boys joining the Navy as insufficient and unsuitable. The lads of that era can thank the Duke for the improvement that took place in the meagre ration of dry ship's biscuit and cocoa on which to start a hard morning's work.

It was his enthusiasm to see Scotland flourish that created Scotland's first trade mission ship. With the co-operation of Donaldson Line their ship *Letitia* was fitted out as a great shopping emporium carrying over eighty " lines " from Scottish industry. The mission was an outstanding success, bringing rich orders to

Scotland. The Duke's advice in 1925 might be followed today:
"Why not send out a trade vessel to visit all the large foreign
ports of the seven seas?"

In spite of his eminent service in many spheres, it was only very
late in life, when everyone else had been served, that he became
a Knight of the Thistle. He who was all his life the epitome of a
true knight of Scotland was put last instead of first in the premier
honours line of Scotland.

> Both men were ardent home rulers, and when Bannerman's
> long and fruitless quest for Parliamentary success began he
> was actively encouraged by the Duke. He was given all the
> time he needed for campaigning in the widespread and remote
> hinterlands of Argyll and Inverness-shire. When the Duke
> spoke at meetings, political or non-political, Bannerman would
> drive him there and act as a second pair of ears, taking note
> of questions and helping the Duke to cope with hecklers when
> he misheard. The Duke as a young man had contested elections
> in Suffolk and Stirlingshire before the First World War when
> he was a Tory, but later his opinions changed. He helped to
> form a short-lived Home Rule Party in 1932 with Sir Alexander
> MacEwen and Professor Dewar Gibb, with the aim of winning
> self-government for Scotland without separation. This soon
> became part of a new moderate Scottish National Party, in
> which John MacCormick was a leading light. After the war
> the Duke's signature appeared at the top of MacCormick's
> great Scottish Convention, a home rule petition which gained
> two million supporters.

So strongly did he disapprove of over-centralisation of power
in the hands of the few in Westminster that he forsook the Tory
benches in the House of Lords in 1936 and became a Liberal, sitting
among the few in that august House. He disliked the prevailing
method of ruling Scotland by a single Secretary of State supported
by under secretaries and an "elephantine bureaucracy". He could
not see why other parts of the British Isles should have their own
Ministers answering in responsible fashion for their actions on their
own soil, and not Scotland.

He visited Ulster, Eire and the Isle of Man in a Scottish delegation to find out how self-government operated in these areas, and
the delegation's report contained the following observations:

" The contacts which we have made in Northern Ireland, Eire
and the Isle of Man have supplied us with ample evidence that
self-government not only confers on a nation a more economical,
efficient and progressive home administration, but that it stimulates
the whole moral and intellectual life of the people, calls forth their
native virtues of self-reliance and independence, and brings to
fruition the artistic and spiritual qualities which are present in most
races. We are not making an excessive claim on behalf of our
countrymen when we say that the people of Scotland are at least
as well qualified as those of the countries which we have just visited
to make good use in their own affairs of the benefits of self-
government ".

His article, written in 1933, on self government is still a model
statement of the aims of those who see the need for decentralisation
from congested Westminster government. He sums up : " What we
require is a well thought out industrial policy for Scotland planned
by Scottish people and supported by an effective and sympathetic
Scottish Parliament ". How prescient his thought in the light of
recent belated plans for regionalisation, born of the desperation of
a centralised Parliament choking on its own appetite for power.

It was some time after the Duke became a Liberal that the Tory
Establishment took a wholly unchivalrous and mean-spirited
revenge. They deprived him of his membership of the Carlton Club,
and in later life he would sit in the smoke room of the Reform
Club, cut off from those lifelong friends whose loyalty and understanding were manifest only for those who toed the line. Some of
us would say he was better off without them.

Bannerman became the Duke's factor and farm manager
at a time when British agriculture was at the ebb. Prices in
the depression years were at rock bottom, and to make matters
worse the estate had been saddled with burdensome death
duties when the former Duke died in 1924. Land had been
sold wholesale to pay off the debt, including the Trossachs
and Loch Katrine, Mugdock, and Ben Lomond. Policies which
had once covered 100,000 acres were now reduced to around
12,000 acres. Among the stratagems adopted by Bannerman
to make farming pay was to sell sheep carcases — which
would fetch only shillings at market — door to door. The estate
shepherd John Armstrong did the butchering and the mutton
was sold all round the neighbourhood and even in Glasgow,

until it was discovered that this enterprise was in breach of the law.

The transformation of the park in front of the castle into Buchanan Castle golf course was another brainchild of Bannerman and the Duke's. The remains of Buchanan House, burned in 1850 and by then used as a laundry, stood beside broad meadows dotted with noble trees and indented by the meandering River Endrick. The last effective use of this park had been for training racehorses at the beginning of the century. Bannerman had the house gutted and made into a club house, and brought in the famous James Braid to lay out the course. He himself took great pleasure in finding suitable names for the holes. Now the golf course is one of the estate's biggest revenue-earners.

During the war the castle was turned into a hospital, and it was here that Rudolf Hess was taken after his plane crash-landed in Scotland. Two of the doctors were billeted at the Old Manse and their excitement was great. ("He's mad", declared one unhesitatingly over the breakfast table). The castle itself served as administrative centre and housed operating theatres, while the wards consisted of numerous hastily constructed huts in the grounds. Nominally the Government was obliged to restore the estate to its former condition when peace came, but in the end a lump payment was agreed on and the negotiation of this claim fell to Bannerman when he came home from the Air Ministry. He also had to dispose of the old W.D. buildings for the best price he could get, and this job was tackled with gusto. Some of the huts were sold as they stood and converted into remarkably attractive private houses. A squad of Irish labourers was employed dismantling the rest, and Bannerman sold roofs, doors, windows, baths, basins and sinks all round the neighbourhood.

Before the war Bannerman had built up a good herd of Aberdeen-Angus beef cattle which would shortly have begun to fetch top prices, but while he was away the estate went over to dairying, a decision he regretted. On his return he found that he had to spend pretty heavily to bring the estates back to first-class order. "When I look back on it", says Bob Hay, his assistant in those days, "I thought it was crazy the way he spent money on buildings and improving the land. I came to respect it when I took over and had the benefit of it ".

He was never a head-down-at-the-desk man : Hay remem-

bers that his most concentrated period of office work was when
he was working on the derequisition claim, but at other times
his attendance at the estate office was erratic. There were
other calls on his time. He was away in Inverness for weeks
during his first election campaign there, keeping in touch with
Hay by phone. He would dash off to Stirling for a county
council meeting, which he attended as the local Liberal
member. He was a Forestry Commissioner between 1942 and
1957, setting off one afternoon at two for a meeting that
night in Wales (he got lost in the dark), or declaiming the
Ossianic *Oran Mor* to his fellow commissioners on the top of
a Scottish ben. One of his most valued appointments was
membership of the Hill Land Commission along with, amongst
others, John Hobbs the millionaire Great Glen cattle rancher,
which made far-reaching proposals for the improvement of
cattle farming in the Highlands. At various times he was
chairman of the National Forest Parks in Scotland, chairman
of *An Comunn Gaidhealach* and for ten years chairman of the
Scottish Liberal Party.

Bannerman was not a typical factor. For one thing, he
had no formal training in estate agency. He was open and
friendly in his dealings with tenants. He carried the tang of
the outdoors about him even in the little office at Drymen,
sitting at the table in the plain armchair with a cushion on
its seat, with the breeze from the open window ruffling his
papers and a picture of the Duke in naval uniform on the
wall behind him.

10

A CANTY SINGER

(Canty: Lively, pleasant, cheerful, merry . . .)

THE Mod, the great festival of Gaelic song and culture, came
to Glasgow in October 1921, and was held throughout the
week in the stately St. Andrews Halls — now no more. Hugh
Macphee remembers the occasion . . .

The vast main hall is packed with Highlanders and the big
platform is filled by the gathered choirs and solo competitors,
John Bannerman among them. He is a student at the university,
and his contribution is the *Oran Mor,* the Big Song, a dramatic
rendering of Ossianic legend, part singing, part recitative.

Bannerman's name is called and he rises from his place in
the third row, walks to the rostrum modestly with his head
down. But shyness vanishes as he delivers the *Oran Mor* with
a spirit that is remembered half a century later. " Oh, he was
a hero ", says Macphee. He finishes, bows, and the audience
thunders applause as he makes his way back to his place, head
downcast again.

That performance won him the Gold Medal.

The following year he had even greater success, winning the
Mod's supreme honour, the Gold Medal for solo singing. This
was more unexpected than his triumph in the *Oran Mor,* for
though his light, slightly husky baritone was clear and true,
it was not an outstanding voice. He used to joke that he won
the medal thanks to a thunderstorm. The Mod was held in
Fort William that year, and since there was no large hall
available the main events took place in a large garage covered
by a corrugated iron roof. Bannerman's turn to sing came as
a cloudburst broke, the waters dripping through the roof joints
on to the audience — among whom was probably Ramsay
MacDonald, the Prime Minister — and drumming resonantly
on the tin roof. Shunting engines in the nearby railway yard
added to the background noise.

I had not accounted myself as more than a traditional fireside singer of Gaelic songs, and no one was more surprised than I when Sir Hugh Roberton, the musical judge, said I could sing and gave me top marks. Only then, I suspect, did *other* people think I could sing — a case of giving the dog a good name. When I had won the *Oran Mor*, it was accounted more declamation than pure singing.

It amused me, coming away from the hall after the gold medal to meet friends in the streets coming from other halls who were anxious to know who had won the medal. When I told them, they all registered shocked surprise before they remembered that congratulations were in order.

A Gold Medal winner may not compete in the event again, and therefore Bannerman did not sing in Mod solo competitions after Fort William, when he was only 21. But he attended all the Mods, and as convenor of the Music Committee for many years he was responsible for organising the Mods and conducting them while in session. Ray, too, became deeply involved in Mod administration, although she did not speak Gaelic, and she took on the onerous task of fund-raising for two recent Mods. Bannerman, whose father had been a notable president of An Comunn before the war, became president himself in 1951. The work took him all over the country, to provincial mods in places like Strontian, or Lochgilphead, Ardnamurchan or Lairg, as well as to the big annual national Mods. Even on the biggest Mod occasions, there would be an atmosphere of informality which he found congenial.

I was seated beside Princess Margaret at a final Mod concert. The winning competitors were performing, and when three appeared together on the platform Princess Margaret asked me which item it was. I said it was the winning quartet. " There appears to be a quart missing ", the Princess observed. He turned up — and it might have been better if he had stayed away, as the Princess said with a chuckle, for his voice was off-key.

I remember the Queen Mother, when she was the Duchess of York, attending a crowded ceilidh in the lounge of the Caledonian Hotel. She asked that no special arrangements be made for her and seated herself on a couch which rapidly filled, like all the other seats in the room. Ceilidhs have the Highland open door, and people eventually had to sit on the floor and on the window sills. It was a bit much, however, when a stalwart kilted Highlander, just arrived and seeing a vacant space at her feet, plonked himself down and prepared to use her legs as a backrest. He was hastily and tactfully moved over a little.

Nothing pleased Bannerman more than to find the evening turning into a ceilidh, and this happened sometimes while he was canvassing in Argyll and Inverness-shire. Who will you vote for? an elderly farmer was asked in Inverness-shire. The old man replied : " Ach well, I think I'll vote for Bannerman. Man, he's awful good at the ceilidhs ". Once, at least, his ceilidh was not appreciated. It was late at night at a Perth hotel during the Mod, the staff wanted to get to bed, and the songs finally were silenced by loud and indignant hoovering.

He needed little excuse to sing. One evening he and another speaker whose subject was stained glass windows were to address a men's guild. Somehow he discovered that the stained glass man was an enthusiastic singer too, and that was the end of talk for the evening.

His ceilidhs could be embarrassing for the shy, for he would insist on the tradition that everyone should do a turn. Bob Hay, now factor of Montrose estates and then Bannerman's assistant, was invited with him to the captain's dinner at the Buchanan Castle golf club. After the meal was eaten, Hay was horrified to discover that all present were expected to perform. It was a small company of about a dozen and there was no escape. Someone sang from the *Mikado,* John Bannerman sang a Scots song, the Duke of Montrose, old salt that he was, rendered a sea chanty. Hay, who claims to have no singing voice at all, remembered his school days in Ayrshire and managed to recite a chunk of *Tam o' Shanter.*

Light-hearted, jovial songs suited Bannerman best, and there are still scratched and worn old gramophone records in existence made by him for H.M.V. " I think we would have to use a Scots word to describe him ", says Hugh McPhee. " He was a canty singer ". The songs he sang — in Gaelic and in English — had titles like *Horo, my little old man, The wedding of fair Iain's sister* and *She'll aye be happy.* All are songs that encourage the audience to join in the chorus. Some were his own compositions, the most famous of which is " Eilidh ",

the Gaelic form of Helen, with words by the bard John
Mackenzie. It is still one of the most popular ceilidh songs
wherever Gaels foregather. *Eilidh* was composed as all his
songs were composed — tinkering on the piano with one finger
and noting down the tune in sol-fa, for he did not read music.

One night he burst into the tenement flat near Glasgow
University where his son John was in digs, studying for an
exam the next day. " I've got a tune you might like ", he said,
and proceeded to sing *Eilidh* — the first time it had been
heard. Both men sang it over and over, changing a note or
a phrase here and there until they felt it was just right. There
was no more swotting done that night.

Besides composing tunes, Bannerman avidly translated
Gaelic songs into English and turned pop and folk songs into
Gaelic (which offended some Gaelic purists). He wanted as
many people as possible to share his pleasure in Gaelic music.
And, above all, he saw music as a way to keep the Gaelic
language strong — the principle on which the Mod itself was
founded.

The Mod is the annual gathering of Gaels from a' the airts, held
in a number of towns in Scotland and organised by *An Comunn
Gaidhealach*. It is Scotland's equivalent of the Welsh Eisteddfod,
and though not nearly so large in scale, it is a week of happy
reunion for thousands of Highlanders. It opens with a broadcast
religious service on the Sunday. Throughout the following week
there are oral and singing competitions for juniors and seniors,
culminating in two grand concerts on the Friday night. Tuesday
is the children's day, with their own concert at night sustained by
the prize-winners in the competitions. Thursday is rural day, with
over a score of country choirs as well as solo singers competing.
The finals of the Mod gold medal solo competitions are also decided
that day. Friday is the climax when the more sophisticated choirs
from the big towns compete and the Bard of the year is crowned.

The Mod is not just another musical festival, but the Gaels' shop
window in their endeavour to spread the spoken and written use
of Gaelic throughout Scotland. The more Scots who can become
bilingual, the deeper will be their appreciation of Scotland's heritage
and musical lore. The greater will also be their knowledge of the
Celtic background of their own country. They will learn the
meaning of the Gaelic names which surround them, but which

are a foreign language to them today. Above all, the Scots nation
would find its birthright.

Gaelic has been subjected for so long to a losing battle with
English, and it is only within recent years that bilingualism has
come to be regarded of additional cultural value to the child in
the Highlands. Directors of education like Dr. John MacLean of
Inverness (now retired) are making valiant efforts to give Gaelic
its proper place as the mother tongue in schools in the Gaelic-
speaking areas. Even in Glasgow, Dr. H. Stewart Mackintosh (also
now retired), a native of Sutherland and in his day a great rugby
forward, has introduced the teaching of Gaelic into a number of
primary and secondary schools.

If to know what *la plume de ma tante* means adds something
to a child's understanding, how much more valuable should it be
to the Scots child to know that Auchenshuggle is not just a quaintly
named terminus in Glasgow but was *achadh an t-seagail,* the field
of rye, before the buses rode over it? The late Sir Donald
MacAlister, Principal of Glasgow University, addressed the education committee of *An Comunn Gaidhealach* at a conference on
Highland education. He was a Gaelic speaker, but not fluent, and
is reputed to have spoken seventeen other languages including
English. He declared : " I found I knew more of English as soon
as I knew more than English ". He advocated the teaching of
Gaelic in schools : " Gaelic was not used as it might have been
in my schooling ", he said. " I was the poorer then, I am the
poorer still for the lack of it ".

11

COME IN, GEORGE . . .

ALTHOUGH I had embarked on a career in agriculture, I was
intensely interested in broadcasting in the early 'thirties, and when
the post of Director of Broadcasting in Scotland became vacant
I decided to " have a go ". Not without trepidation, I accepted an
invitation to go to London to see Lord Reith, Director General
of the B.B.C.

I had first seen Lord Reith in black university robes — and with
arms spread and gown flapping he was indeed a frightening,
draconian figure. This was the image I had in mind when I was
ushered into the presence, in his leather-covered sanctum. It was
not a bright room, and with the sombre hue of his dark suit, his
black beetling brows, he towered over me the very picture from
my imagination. I sat while he flapped his great arms and legs
from one end of the room to the other, sometimes pausing to take
short circles before swooping in on me for the kill.

" Do you know anything about the Disruption? " he asked.
" When was it? "

I thought desperately . . . Something to do with a breakaway
in the Church of Scotland, but when? Dates I never knew much
of. Hopelessly I murmured something about last century.

He moved away, knowing he had me groggy, but only to swoop
back and snap out, " Who was Dr. Chalmers? "

That finished me. I went down, gasping incoherently that he
was an Edinburgh man. In all my religious instruction at school
I had more chance of knowing the background of Pope Pius X
than of the divine who had altered the course of Scottish church
history.

Sadly, Lord Reith went into a dark corner of his room and sat
down. In kindly fashion he asked me about things I could talk
about, like the Highlands and rugby, but he and I both knew we
were just waiting for the tea to come.

That was the end of my hopes of guiding the development of

81

broadcasting in Scotland, but shortly afterwards I started what was to become a lifelong association with radio and then television as a performer. It happened through my interest in Gaelic and Gaelic folksong. I remembered broadcasting Gaelic programmes from dark little rooms in an old tenement building at the north-west corner of Blythswood Square, Glasgow, now replaced by new office buildings. This was the headquarters of B.B.C. (Scotland), as the official title went — I always resented that Scotland should be in brackets. These were happy pioneering days of make-do and men in broadcasting, and the folksong and literature of Gaelic began to be heard by many Scots folk who previously have found it difficult even to recognise the native language of their country. As the Glaswegian is reputed to have said to his companion on overhearing a conversation in Gaelic on a tramcar : " Yon's Russian ! "

After moving to Broadcasting House in Queen Margaret Drive, in the West End of the city, the status and quality of Gaelic broadcasting advanced steadily, chiefly due to the crusading zeal of Hugh Macphee, a native of Ballachulish who was in charge of Gaelic broadcasting. Under his direction, twice a week for three years, I taught the great public of Scotland Gaelic. My pupil George in the series was the late Archie Hendry, a splendid broadcaster and a kindly man whose friends were legion. The popularity of these Gaelic lessons, spiced with fun and humorous incident, exceeded wildest expectations. Where it had been calculated that perhaps 50,000 or at most 100,000 people might listen and learn, the equivalent of the modern TAM ratings showed that eventually over a million people listened twice per week. A hard core of these were serious learners, the rest liked the sound of the Gaelic and enjoyed the humorous English asides. The secret of the success of these Gaelic lessons was that we sugared the pill a little, breaking down the barrier of prejudice against the unknown which in the past has been the source of the Lowlander's lack of sympathy for Gaelic.

For many years after these radio lessons stopped I was greeted by strangers in shops and in the street* with my opening Gaelic phrase " *Thig a stigh, George* ", come in, George — a short phrase which, by the way, was criticised by some Gaelic purists, who can

* And once by a heckler as Bannerman stepped forward to address a meeting in an Inverness-shire election campaign.

seldom let well alone. They were technically right, of course, when they pointed out that instead of using *stigh,* which means " in the house ", I should have used *steach* for " into the house ". My version, however, is ordinary usage among most Gaelic speakers, except in parts of the outer islands where Gaelic still retains much of its pristine correctness and generous spread of vocabulary. *Smath sin,* that's good, was another common phrase which was picked up by the public. It became household Gaelic throughout the Lowlands, for the pronunciation is exactly the same as the term in great vogue at the time among teenagers — " smashin' ".

The overwhelming response that the series received caused quite severe embarrassment to the B.B.C. printing establishment, which found itself using an inordinate amount of its time printing the illustrated booklets for study alongside the broadcasts. Five thousand were originally printed, but this and the later more advanced lesson books had to be printed in many editions to satisfy the great demand. That these lessons have never been resumed, or a new series put on the air, is quite inexplicable. Individuals and interested bodies such as *An Comunn Gaidhealach* have voiced a demand through the intervening years, but these have met with official silence quite impervious to suggestion or request. Can it be that B.B.C. Scotland is confined to such an extent, financial and otherwise, that no place can be found for a programme basic to Scotland's history and heritage, and more than acceptable to the Scottish people?

My active interest in Gaelic broadcasting was equalled by the zest with which I took part from time to time on the panel of *Matter of Opinion.* This splendid radio discussion programme was produced latterly by Roddie MacLean, now director of audio-visual studies at the universities of Glasgow and Strathclyde, and chaired by Noel Stevenson, who was later for a period managing director of Scottish Television.

Lively as the programme was, the discussions at dinner afterwards when the panel let down their hair were possibly even more enlightening and entertaining. If these events could have been recorded without the knowledge of the participants they would have surpassed many a broadcast entertainment!

One memorable occasion took place after a *Matter of Opinion* broadcast from the Isle of Islay. I was not on the panel on that occasion, but had been compering a ceilidh which went on the air immediately after the discussion programme. On the panel were Jack House, friend, journalist and author, and Eric Linklater, man of letters, Orcadian and supreme broadcaster for whom I have a great respect, not only because of his attainments and originality but also because of his enthusiasms. William Ross, later to be Scottish Secretary in the Labour Government, and the advocate Lionel Daiches, Q.C., were also taking part.

After dining well at the White Hart Hotel in Port Ellen, we all foregathered in the Victorian furnishings of the sitting room there. Chairman Noel Stevenson no longer worried what was said or who said what, and a few friends dropped in as they are wont to do when the ceilidh magnet draws. I had just completed an impassioned rendering of the great Ossianic *Oran Mor,* the Big Song. It was *The Banners of the Fenians,* describing the battle between the *Lochlannaich* or Scandinavians and the Fenians — and if ever Linklater had heard anything to equal the vital quality of a Norse saga, this was it! The Viking spirit bequeathed him by a long ancestry of marauding Norsemen was roused to fighting pitch, and seizing the Victorian brass coal scuttle (fortunately empty) he up-ended it on his head for a helmet. Clutching the big brass poker in his right hand, he leapt on to the fireguard and proceeded to declaim his version of a heroic saga. Poker held aloft and eyes flashing from below the rim of the brass bucket, no Viking could have looked fiercer.

Matter of Opinion became a splendid link between the B.B.C. and its Scottish listeners over the years. It was a safety valve for ventilating many social and economic questions affecting Scotland, and repercussions of the views expressed sometimes reached the national press, moulded public opinion and created valuable Scottish lobbies in Westminster itself. Then, suddenly, came the decree that the programme was to cease, issued in the name of the Postmaster General — and who was to question such a source of power? Tom Johnston, then chairman of the Broadcasting Council for Scotland, resented the *diktat* and threatened resignation. But to no avail. We were told that Scottish B.B.C. officials could do nothing but give support to the edict, and in justification they made noises that the listening figures were going down. Justified or not, I suspect that the decision to close this valve of Scottish opinion was political. Opinions were becoming embarrassing to the central Government, and the fact that the rival English programme *Any Questions* was not taken off and continues hale and hearty to the present day seems to confirm that there was discrimination against Scottish interests.

It is an unhappy fact that Scotland is especially vulnerable to the standardising effect of programmes based on English incident and life, heard or seen daily for years throughout Britain. Why is it that the Scottish people must accept programmes like *The Archers* which have an English bias, while equivalent programmes of a Scottish character, with the notable exception of *Dr. Finlay's Casebook,* are in the main accounted provincial and fit only to be shown in Scotland? I am afraid it reflects the power of majority rule to which Scotland is subjected in broadcasting as well as in other spheres. I believe we should demand the right to opt *in* to the English programme network rather than be content, as at present, to have only a limited right to opt *out.* In the meantime I fear that though the charters for sound and television obviously reflect the desire to avoid the evil of centralisation while retaining its good, the Scottish broadcasting council wages a losing battle trying to maintain " the distinctive culture, language, interests and tastes " of the people of Scotland against the overwhelming power and economic influence of England.

I also regret that Scots producers of first-class calibre, now and in the past — men like James Crampsey, Finlay J. Macdonald and the Orcadian Archie P. Lee, who have given the public so much worthwhile drama and documentary — should have had such a limited horizon of appreciation, with comparatively few opportunities to make productions in Scotland because the purse strings are in London and most of what they do produce is accounted parochial by the standards of the London English. The B.B.C. in Scotland has therefore to make feverish hay while the sun shines.

Now and again, however, there has been enough money to produce and present programmes of Scottish character and origin. One with which I was intimately connected was the series of radio plays based on Neil Munro's novel *John Splendid,* which found great favour due to the skill and sympathy of the producer, James Crampsey. Urged, I think, by Hugh Macphee, he took a chance and put me in the big title role. Any acting ability I had came via some efforts I had made with Gaelic plays, but Neil Munro expressed better than most Scottish novelists the character of the Highlands in war and peace — and so I think I won the professional approval of Crampsey.

To Elizabeth Bannerman, sitting up late on Sunday nights to hear her father in the play, John Bannerman *was* John Splendid, and when at the end she heard his horse clip-clopping into the distance her eyes filled with tears, for she thought he was gone for good. It was a brilliant stroke of casting, for Bannerman's warm, expansive personality fitted the role exactly : John Splendid, a poor cousin of the marquis, "with little schooling, but some wit and gentlemanly parts . . . a fellow you would never weary of although you tramped with him in a thousand glens ". John Splendid was a devil-may-care mercenary soldier of the seventeenth century, home in Inveraray from the Continental wars, only to become engaged in high adventure in the disturbances called the little wars of Lorn. Bannerman, rehearsing in his kilt, kicking his heel back in irritation when he fluffed a line, loved the part and almost lived it. All the same, James Crampsey remembers the first read-through as deplorably bad — maybe emphasised by his own doubts about the wisdom of giving a talented amateur the star part. Bannerman's experience until then was limited to performing at the Gaelic Ceilidhs or in the Gaelic plays attributed to his uncle, which were presented in the little theatre at the Athenaeum. In order to bring the final leave-taking scene at Inveraray to life, Bannerman rounded up as many of the young B.B.C. secretaries as he could find and hugged them in his outstretched arms. One girl had a bruise on her forehead to mark the force of his big embrace.

Besides John Splendid, he appeared in numerous radio plays. Another for which he seemed perfectly fitted was an emotional drama about a family of Highland exiles making a new life on the eastern shore of Canada. Bannerman played the father, an old man yearning for his homeland across the waves. The climax comes when a ceilidh in their little house is interrupted by a stranger bringing a pathetic bundle of clothes, and the news that the old man's son has been drowned at sea. The father reaches for the Bible and starts to read the 23rd Psalm : " The Lord is my shepherd . . . " " Say it in the old Scots tongue ", his wife interrupts, and in the original version of the play he repeats it in what the Canadian author assumed to be Scots doric. Neither Bannerman nor Crampsey liked it, and then they had a brainwave. Bannerman, in gravel voice, solemnly intoned the Psalm in Gaelic, with heart-tugging effect.

Later Bannerman had parts in several television plays. But by this time he was finding it a strain to learn lines, he was ill at ease in the medium, and in one play he felt conscious of some patronising by more sophisticated actors from London.

He himself had a bluff contempt for what he considered the hot-house atmosphere of the acting profession in the south, and therefore deterred his daughter Janet from going to R.A.D.A. and making her career on the stage, although she had appeared with him in radio plays.

He was entirely at home, however, in the short, informal fireside ceilidhs he conducted for Scottish Television as the traditional *fear an tigh,* the man of the house. " I always considered myself a fireside singer ", he has said, and the intimate setting of the ceilidh house in which he introduced singers like Alasdair Gillies and Evelyn Campbell was congenial. There was the authentic informality about these programmes. The music was provided by an accordionist, and Bannerman would have his black Labrador dog at his side. The programmes started with Bannerman going over to light the fire. In one programme the fire was seen to flicker before he reached it. " Instant peat ", he remarked calmly, and convulsed the camera crew. Another off-the-cuff remark had to be cut before transmission : the programmes were gradually being put out later and later in the evening, and at the close of a recording he announced, " We'll see you next week after the Epilogue ".

The song which opened each one of the series, *Over the islands we will go,* had a special significance for Bannerman, for both words and music were written by his father. It is a jaunty, lilting Gaelic song which goes back to his boyhood when his father and he used to stroll along the sands on the island of Tiree, his father telling him about the islands scattered around them, their names and their histories.

Each ceilidh would include one or two popular songs which he and John Gillies, father of Alasdair Gillies, had translated into Gaelic. *Red River Valley* was one of the most successful, and even *Glasgow belongs to me* appeared in one programme in Gaelic.

In one series each programme was extended to include a short Gaelic lesson — harking back to the days of " Come in, George " — in which Jack House was the pupil. At first House was taken aback at the unorthodox, take-it-as-it-comes way in which Bannerman approached the lessons. House signed the contract and was told when to report for the first rehearsal. At the due time, 2 p.m. on a Saturday, he reported to the Theatre Royal studio in Glasgow, sought out Bannerman and

told him that he hadn't yet received a script. Bannerman
guffawed. " Well, I'm not surprised ", he said, " because there
isn't a script ". And so, with no more preparation than a
discussion on where the scene should be set — in the grocer's
shop or in the village street, for example — and a quick run
through before the recording, the programme went out for
thirteen weeks. House says it was good entertainment, but it
taught him no Gaelic. So many people approached him in the
street and chattered away in Gaelic that the only phrase to
stick in his mind was the Gaelic for " I don't understand ".

From the day of my ill-starred interview in the early 'thirties
I had not met Lord Reith until I sat next to him at the centenary
of the Glasgow Academical Club already referred to in my chapter
of rugby reminiscences. There I reminded him of our last meeting,
and in expansive after-dinner atmosphere he told me of his envy
of my International rugby caps, and of how he determined to be
a full-back and get his cap for Scotland when he went to London
before 1914 and played for London Scottish. I am sure that had
not the war intervened he would have succeeded. But like his
fellow Academicals in Scotland he went to war — a war which
took fearful toll on the Accies XV of 1913-14 (captained by Arthur
Laird), all of whom went to war, eight of whom were killed and
six wounded. Reith himself was seriously wounded.

When I sat down after making my speech at the dinner, Lord
Reith leaned over and said, " You know, if I had to make my
decision again about you it might be a different one ". He, and no
doubt I, have mellowed. If only I could have made a speech to
him on rugby instead of the Disruption at that fateful interview
in the 'thirties, who knows? There might have been no need to
put Scotland in brackets.

12

FEAR AN TIGH — MAN OF THE HOUSE

THE small boats moored in the bay were gay with bunting as
John Bannerman and his bride drove home from their honey-
moon in 1931. When they reached the village of Balmaha
their car was taken in tow by a gang of sturdy men —
employees of the Duke of Montrose at Buchanan Castle —
and drawn up the steep brae to the Old Manse, where they
were met by the Duke and Duchess. The solid, white-walled,
stone-built house set in its own grounds overlooking the broad
reach of Loch Lomond, was to be their home for the rest of
their married life. Here they raised a family of four — John
and Calum, Janet and Elizabeth.

Bannerman was away from the Old Manse only during the
war, when he worked as a lands officer for the Air Ministry.
At first he had applied for a commission in the Cameron
Highlanders, the regiment in which his cousins had served
and died during the 1914-18 war, but his letter to the War
Office was never answered. Then he tried the Air Force in
the hope of becoming a pilot, but he was too old to be
considered. They said the only flying job he could get at
nearly 40 was as a gunner, and since he had four young
children he was ruled out for that, too. Bannerman finally
wrote to Sir Archibald Sinclair (later Lord Thurso), the
Liberal M.P. and Air Minister in the Churchill Government,
who offered him a post in the Ministry. This involved travelling
all over Britain from his base in London seeking sites for
airfields, with powers of confiscation if necessary. There was
one blistering row with a Scottish lord who had to be forced
into handing over the carefully tended park in front of his
castle. Bannerman twice arrived back in London to find his
digs demolished in the Blitz.

Later in the war he worked for the Air Ministry in Aberdeen, sharing a room with his daughter Janet, who went to

the High School there. There he helped her with her home-work, sometimes slipping out with her to a meeting of An Comunn with a conspiratorial air because she ought to have been in bed. His office was in an attic just down the road, and at lunchtime Janet would wait outside the building, looking up at the window until he looked out and waved, the signal that he was ready to leave.

While in Aberdeen he wrote his novel, with Janet sitting up in her bed pretending she was writing one too. But though it was a labour of love, it never reached a publisher. The only copy of the manuscript, carefully written out in longhand, disappeared when his brief-case was stolen from a night train to London. He made several fresh starts, but his heart was no longer in the work and it was never completed. Much of the story was based on his own childhood experience in the islands, and Calum, the hero, falls into a dung heap chasing a feather toy just as the little John Bannerman did. Now all that remains of the novel is a diagram on a dog-eared page with the words " MacDonalds of Machair Farm " at the top, " Calum's schooldays " below it, and the sketch of a subsequent career that looks like wish-fulfillment : 14 (presumably Calum's age) Oban High School; 20 Glasgow University; Member of Parliament; Reform.

For the great part of his life Bannerman's dress was the tweed jacket and MacDonald tartan kilt (though Forbes is the Bannerman tartan. Bannerman claimed to be three-quarters MacDonald because both his mother and his maternal grand-mother were MacDonalds). In London, electioneering in Paisley, and generally later in life he would wear a plain suit, but at home and on familiar territory it had to be the kilt. One of his son John's earliest memories is of clinging to the pleats as he trotted beside his father through head-high bracken on one of the Duke's shoots over the farm. Elizabeth, as a child, thought her father looked odd if he wore trousers. The kilt, being a practical outdoor garment, failed him only once, and that occurred during a short-lived interest in bee-keeping. Suddenly he burst into view, running across the yard from the hives with his arms flailing and cursing mightily, chased by a swarm of angry bees. That painful incident brought his ambitions as an apiarist to an abrupt end.

There was always music at the Old Manse, with the family given every encouragement to sing — and if Highlanders were guests the night would turn into a ceilidh. Bannerman tried out his own tunes on the rosewood grand piano in the corner of the lounge, and — impressed by Andy Stewart's singing of *The Scottish Soldier* — brought Stewart there to run over the Gaelic songs he had turned into English. The Stewart family of girls came too, and Bannerman got them to amuse themselves by hunting through the neighbouring wood for the elephants he swore lived there. Trying to soothe the girls' indignation when they failed to find any proved more difficult. His musical accomplishments also included some skill with the humble Jew's harp, a favourite poor man's instrument in the Western Isles of his youth and a great success with the children. His taste in music was simple and straightforward : he liked anything with a recognisable tune, whether it was a pop hit or classical, but he could find no pleasure in the more austere modern music, for example, and was suspicious of those who claimed they could. Negro spirituals, in which he saw an affinity to Gaelic music, were old favourites. He was often worried in case the music he wrote for his songs was unconsciously borrowed from the tunes he knew, and used to ask John or Janet if they had heard them before.

All the children were brought up to sing and to take part in the Mod, although Elizabeth was the only one who did so as an adult. But their joint music-making was not always harmonious. His piano-playing by ear was erratic and he could not master some keys, with the result that Elizabeth sometimes found herself expected to sing too high or too low. She also disagreed with him when he insisted on the Mod ruling that Gaelic pronunciation should always take precedence over the musical phrasing, and a recital could break up in strenuous argument between father and daughter.

But Bannerman was proud of Elizabeth's success as a folk singer. On her birthday the family went out to dinner at Ferrari's restaurant in Glasgow, and Elizabeth, who had not yet received her present from him, was kept on tenterhooks all evening. At last when they had finished their meal he gleefully signalled the waiter who brought in from the kitchen the present she had most wanted — a guitar. (His choice in presents was erratic. When the family were clamouring for skates he arrived home with a bundle of assorted pairs — all ice-hockey skates and none measured to fit. The children had to sit down and find out by trial and error which boots fitted

whose feet best.) His enthusiasm for Elizabeth's singing made
her nervous and she made him promise not to attend her
competitions at an Inverness Mod. He cheated, of course, and
when she ran to tell him she had won he greeted her with
a broad smile — he already knew.

Competitions, in music as in anything else, appealed to his
nature. Practising with Elizabeth, he'd make believe they were
already at the Mod and it would be a case of " one, two, three
and in " in real earnest. At one of Janet's school plays he
slipped back stage to find her suffering from stage fright,
squeezed her arm comfortingly and said : " The others haven't
a look in ".

It was the same with sports and games which he played
with good humour and gusto, but always with a determination
to win, and this applied to anything from club rugby to
family tennis on the blaes court (now converted to a hen run)
at the Old Manse. He developed a boisterous game of tennis
at Oxford, with an armoury of killer strokes which owed
nothing to style and orthodoxy. He often quoted the occasion
when Ray threw her racket at him in exasperation after he
had sneaked a winner past her and then laughed uproariously
at her discomfiture.

His quick eye and aptitude for physical things served him
well in any sport he took up. Though he was never to be
seen on the practice greens, he was a good golfer who could
hit a ball straight and true and far. He was an enthusiastic
curler. He was a good shot when he went out on the hills
with his favourite spaniel Ille for pheasant or rabbit. And
though he was never a fly fisher, he would spend whole
mornings fishing with rod and line from a boat in a Highland
loch or in the bay off Brodick when he was a guest at the
castle.

The Bannerman family seldom took an organised holiday.
When John and Janet went to France on exchange he swept
up the drive one evening blasting furiously on the car horn
(three toots were his customary signal to the family that he
had arrived) with a caravan in tow. Nothing would do but
that Ray, Calum and Elizabeth should set off on a caravan
holiday with him that very night. Car journeys were always
shortened by lusty sing-songs, and if the children had to wait
in the car for any reason — if Ray was shopping, for example

— he devised a game for them to play, inventing characters and stories for the passers-by on the pavement.

Bannerman studiously instructed the children on their family history, hoping that they would pass it on as he had learned it from his own father. When Elizabeth was eight years old he took John and her on a sentimental journey back to South Uist, the island where his father was born — and where the ruined walls of the Bannerman home still stand. While there they crossed the sound to go to the North Uist games and missed the last ferry back. Eventually they found a boat-man to take them across, but he turned out to be drunk and stranded them on a sandbank in the pitch darkness. The rest of the night was spent in the open waiting for the tide to rise, with the boatman jovially but ineffectually shining his torch up into the night sky.

Ray and Janet remember another night spent under the stars, this time from choice. The three of them were driving south after coming off the last ferry from Skye, where they had been electioneering. The night was velvety and moonlit and the whim took Bannerman to stop the car and sleep for a while on the heather. Who else would have done it?

13

OUR MAN BANNERMAN

SOME time during the early 'thirties Bannerman became drawn into politics, a passionate brand of politics in which the theme of home rule for Scotland came to dominate the latter half of his life. He was a politician without guile who scorned manoeuvre or intrigue. His ambition was to give the ordinary people of the Highlands and islands a fair share in the affluent society, and he abominated the pin-striped prejudice of Westminster and Whitehall which he blamed for denying them it. He campaigned with a fervour which won vociferous approval from packed village halls in the Highlands where so many of his campaigns were fought.

He fought seven campaigns in all between 1945 and 1964, the first five in the vast Highland constituencies of Argyll and Inverness-shire involving long, tiring journeys by sea and over difficult terrain where communications were uncertain at the best of times. Electioneering might take him away from home for weeks at a time or it could mean tedious day trips north extending into the early hours. He was usually accompanied by Ray, the organising dynamo of a remarkable political twosome. Organised Liberal support in the early days in Argyll was sparse or non-existent, and they and their few helpers would dash out into the country first thing in the morning to stick up posters, often returning the same evening to address the meetings they advertised. Bannerman, to the dismay of orthodox campaigners, would happily spend hours tramping for miles to the head of a glen to talk with a handful of shepherds — hardly worthwhile in votecatching terms.

Because of his big, extrovert personality and his reputation as a ceilidh singer, unscrupulous opponents in Inverness-shire put it about that a Bannerman political meeting was no more than a glorified ceilidh and that he was turning the political platform into a music hall stage. There wasn't a jot of truth in it, but the smear gained credence. From this it was simple to take a further step and suggest that he was too fond of the bottle, whence arose the tales that he had been carried drunk to bed in this, that or the other hotel. In truth, John Bannerman needed no strong drink to stoke his enthusiasm or restore his energies, and he remained abstemious to the end of his days. But some of the mud stuck, as Russell Johnston discovered when he became candidate for Inverness-shire in place of Bannerman. It took the threat of legal action to prevent the calumny from being transferred to the new man. Johnston found he had to style his campaign deliberately on a lower key in order to escape the anti-Bannerman backlash.

In these Highland constituencies meetings were crowded and never dull, though they were not always good-humoured. One held in Skye — which contains a large proportion of "elite" Highlanders — became particularly acrimonius as a local military gentleman (retd.) directed a string of hostile questions at Bannerman. "That's a damned lie", shouted the chairman at last, the chairman being minister of the kirk in which the military man was an elder. Bannerman contented himself, once the questioner had finally sat down, with the growl, "He can go to hell!"

Ray shared with him the long, cold journeys, the hours in uncomfortable halls, the snatched meals — and the speaking engagements. The family, too, would take part, Janet taking over the loudspeaker van or acting as holding speaker at one hall, spinning out the time until her long overdue father arrived from another.

The posters throughout Inverness-shire proclaimed "Our man Bannerman", although it annoyed him if anyone suggested that it was his personality rather than his policies which won votes. It was his dearest wish to speak for the Highlands in the House of Commons and three times he came close to succeeding. In 1955 he polled only 966 votes less than the victor — beaten, he believed, by the postal vote. Yet he insisted on abdicating from the seat in order to stand in the Paisley by-election of 1961, leaving the way open for Russell Johnston to capture Inverness-shire for the Liberals in the 1964 general election. Only his immense prestige as chairman of the Scottish Liberal Party, a post he held from 1955 until 1965, enabled him to overrule the party executive and stand for this apparently lost cause when no one else was available.

The 17,542 votes he amassed at Paisley, reducing a solid
Labour majority of more than 9,000 to a whisper, astonished
everyone including himself, and he then felt morally bound
to stay.

Defeat always disappointed him bitterly, though he put a
brave face on it. He would be unusually quiet for a week or
two, reading a lot and saying little, with Ray diplomatically
quiet too. Then suddenly he would bounce back and be ready
to fight again.

After the general election of 1964 he stepped down —
though for a fleeting moment in the following year it seemed
just possible that the old warhorse would saddle up again and
gallop into the Borders for a by-election in Roxburgh, Selkirk
and Peebles. It was not to be, and in the bitter March of
1965, snow glistening on his bushy eyebrows, he was barn-
storming for the young David Steel — the Boy David, he
christened him in the phrase headlined by the *Scottish Daily
Express* on the morning of Steel's famous victory.

Some say that Bannerman, too, might have won the
Borders, where prejudice could not be whipped up against him
as in Inverness. His great past as a rugby player won him
huge audiences in this stronghold of the game. He packed
Hawick Town Hall and the great eve-of-poll rally at the
Kelso cinema thundered applause for his last speech in the
campaign. " Remember ", he told these rugby enthusiasts, " the
poll closes at nine o'clock tomorrow. If you see a Tory coming
after that just blow your whistle! "

As he watched the bundles of votes pile up for Steel someone remarked that in his long career this was the first time
he had been present at a count when he was on the winning
side. Did he regret that the votes were not for him? According
to Jeremy Thorpe there were tears in his eyes when he said,
" If this laddie gets in it'll all have been worthwhile ". The
next day Bannerman, Ray, David and Judy Steel lunched
together in a Galashiels hotel. David Steel, somewhat deflated
after the first heady excitement, noticed that Bannerman was
still jubilant. It should have been John, he thought to himself.
It was unjust that a stripling of 26 should succeed where
this man who had fought so many battles and come so close
had failed.

But if Bannerman felt the pangs of envy, he kept it close
to his heart.

What took me naïvely into politics in the early 'thirties was the spectacle of shameful unemployment and the sorry trail of Scotsmen — many of them Highlanders — away from their homes in scores of thousands, scattering to the four corners of the earth in search of the jobs and self respect denied them at home. I knew that 59 Liberals in the House of Commons had tabled a work plan for Britain in 1929 in order to create real wealth in the shape of new roads, bridges and housing and to take some of the millions of craftsmen and workmen off the dole. My gorge rose against the two power parties, Tory and Socialist, for combining to throw the plan out and so condemn millions of men and women to years of degredation. It was to wrest power from a couldn't-care-less Westminster Government through the Liberal policy of home rule for Scottish domestic affairs that made me decide to fight as a Liberal on the hustings and endeavour to bring constructive legislation to bear on the special problems of the Highland people and Scotland. To win a seat in the House of Commons would have been easy for me as a Socialist or Tory. But I had no wish to go to Westminster except in protest against the continuing refusal to provide for the ordinary social and economic needs of the Highland and Scottish people. I knew it would be ineffective to voice protests without the opportunity of taking them to the floor of the the House of Commons.

It was not until the General Election of 1935 that I took my first hesitant steps on to the hustings in support of John MacCormick, who was standing as a Scottish Nationalist candidate in Inverness-shire. I like to think that I served my apprenticeship with the finest political journeyman of his generation in Scotland. John MacCormick in appearance was a small, quiet, dour Scots lawyer, but the warm Highland blood of the island of Mull coursed in his veins, and when he stood alone on the platform it seemed that he grew physically in stature. Succinct, humorous, knowledgeable, statesmanlike — no audience in Highlands or Lowlands could doubt that it was " King John " speaking to them. What a spokesman he would have been for Scotland in the House of Commons, yet in the end the Establishment crushed him. He loved Scotland and her people o'ermuch to allow him to compromise with Tory or Socialist. Yet he was no extremist. All he asked was that Scotland be given the right to manage her own affairs and become a working partner in the United Kingdom instead of meekly accepting the contemptible status of sleeping partner accorded by Westminster.

His detractors were many and vicious. In the gutter coinage of the political quislings, who may have been few in number but were powerful in their possession and influence, he was accused of expediency (along with other vices). They said that at Glasgow University he had been Labour, that he had become a Scottish Nationalist and finally a Liberal. Politics is a dirty game, and the bigger the lie the more eagerly it is circulated. No man in his lifetime stood more loyal for Scotland than MacCormick. If he was Labour at the University it was because Kier Hardie Socialism had home rule for Scotland at its heart. When he was chairman of the Scottish National Party separatism was neither its aim nor in its constitution, though there were separatists in the party. It was his very consistency that made him keep searching, and latterly as a Liberal he found the true home for his beliefs. Perhaps his greatest achievement was the two million signatures he obtained for the Scottish Convention petition for home rule for Scotland. This was contemptuously set aside by Mr. Attlee and his Labour Government. No doubt many of the signatories continued to vote for the Socialist party that had kicked them in the teeth. It is a sad commentary that a generation of Scots were blind to the stature of the prophet in their midst, and deaf to the wisdom of his words.

However, his meetings everywhere in Inverness-shire in 1935 were crowded and enthusiastic — although one I attended with him in the court house of Portree in the Isle of Skye ended on an uncharacteristic sour note. The fervour was mounting and there could be few in the crowded audience who were not inspired by MacCormick's vision of a new Highlands. Then a supporting speaker unwisely declared that the British empire had been established in the name of religion " at the point of a pistol ". Ministers of the Kirk whom I had not noticed before jumped to their feet from various parts of the courthouse to denounce the speaker with righteous wrath. Gone in a twinkling was the friendliness and enthusiasm. One can say many things unchallenged at a political meeting. But to suggest in the courthouse at Portree that religion took a pistol in its hand to further imperial aggrandisement, and to say so in the presence of ministers, and presumably many of their elders, is asking for trouble !

In spite of the encouraging support which gathered round MacCormick he was defeated at the poll, and thereafter he turned to Liberalism for the expression of his beliefs. My own political development followed the same path and I was adopted prospective Liberal candidate for Argyll. In 1938 I set to, along with Ray, to nurse this huge constituency which stretches from Kinlochleven to

Campbeltown, from Dunoon to Oban, and which includes Tiree, Coll, Mull, Islay and Jura in its many clusters of offshore islands.

The county of Argyll seemed to me to epitomise all the evils, economic and social, to which the Highlands had fallen heir since the evictions. It is a county of lairds and bonnet lairds, and feudalism stands guard against the invasion of any other " ism " except its blood brother Conservatism. Fred Macquisten, K.C., was the Tory Member of Parliament during the 'thirties, a man of high personal attainments and forthright in his opinions within the limits of his party's interests. It was said that he was legal adviser to a brewery combine and made a stump speech regularly on their behalf in Parliament. He courageously and diligently took up individual cases of hardship and injustice among his constituents. But he never used his undoubted powers of intellect and expression to bring any comprehensive redress to the problems of depopulation, unemployment and transport deficiencies which were such obvious symptoms of decline in Argyll, as in the Highlands generally.

Some time after Fred Macquisten died early in 1940 I was invited by prominent members of the Tory party in Argyll to be his successor, provided I became a National Liberal. The offer no doubt was made in good faith and my public refusal should perhaps have been less blunt. But to consider that I, a Liberal, should become a Tory — and a dishonest one at that — in order to get a safe seat in Parliament seemed to me an insult and I rejected the offer forcefully. Then the Tories brought Major Duncan McCallum back from Egypt after an absence abroad of some 30 years. Major McCallum had no direct knowledge of what had happened over that period in Argyll or in Scotland and had a sorry time of it during the by-election he fought in April 1940. In view of the war and the truce agreed between the parties I decided not to go forward. But William Power of the old Glasgow *Evening News,* a great protagonist of Scotland's rights, stood as a Scottish Nationalist at short notice and polled more than 7,000 votes to McCallum's 12,000.

A black-faced sheep, it is said in some parts of Scotland, if labelled Tory and made to bleat at regular intervals, would be returned to Parliament with a thumping majority. I attended Major McCallum's eve-of-poll meeting in Dunoon and was sorry to see such a pleasant man so vulnerable. He made a ten-minute speech, said to be the one he had used throughout his campaign; uninspired and futile. Then came the questions. McCallum at first declined to rise to his feet and attempt to answer any of them,

and for this he was shouted at. His little agent tried to answer
for him, but he was howled down. One questioner asked Major
McCallum for his policy on transport in Argyll, a most pertinent
question, perhaps the most urgent in the economics of living in the
country. The major remained seated for perhaps a minute before
the uproar made him get up. His reply was : " I have been studying
this problem urgently, but my policy is not yet complete. I can
assure the questioner I will do my utmost to help in these transport
difficulties ". Neither he nor the Tories, then or since, have had a
comprehensive policy for this the most vexed problem of the
Highlands.

There are no constituencies anywhere in Britain more in need of
expert and devoted attention in Parliament than the Highland
constituencies, yet until the election of 1964 they remained this
generation's equivalent of the rotten burghs. Orkney and Shetland
freed itself in 1950 and has blessed the name of Jo Grimond ever
since, as have millions of people throughout Britain.

Major McCallum had fine personal qualities. Ably helped by his
wife, he was a diligent domestic member, but it was utterly outside
his Conservative faith to bring about any comprehensive redress
for the problems which have made Argyll and the Highlands the
most backward area in Britain in the twentieth century. At the time
of writing, Michael Noble, former Secretary of State for Scotland,
represents Argyll, fighting a rearguard action for the Tories in the
Highlands — the only one left to cover their retreat.*

Having stood aside in 1940, I returned to party politics to fight
the General Election of 1945. With little or no organisation to help
us, Ray and I travelled the length and breadth of Argyll, voyaging
over the stormy waters between the islands, often in darkness. Once,
crossing between Tiree and Coll in a small fishing boat, we had to
hang on for dear life and at the same time try to help the two
stalwart fisherman-crofters from Caolas, Tiree, as we struggled
against wind and tide and the waves which broke over our bows.

My meeting that night was at Arinagour, the Sheiling of the
Goats, the main port of Coll. A gathering of enthusiastic men and
women from all parts of the island crowded into the classroom of
the school. There was hardly space for the desk that served as my

---

* Mr. Noble, Minister of Trade in the Heath Government, is less lonely
now. He was reinforced at the 1970 General Election when J. H. N. Gray
polled less than a third of the votes cast in Ross and Cromarty and was
elected Conservative member by a majority of 801.

platform. The late General Stewart was in the chair. General Stewart, as he declared himself, was not a Liberal. But he was proprietor of Coll and so he took the chair at any important meeting on the island.

My main representative on the island at that time was the Rev. Donald Robertson, later minister on the Isle of Eigg, a real champion of the people. A man like Robertson would have been a godsend in stiffening the resistance to the evictions a century before, unlike the "will of God" ministers of the time. Small in stature, he had the heart of a lion, a fearless scourge of those who exploited the people, and was a credit to the Church of Scotland.

Old and young sat crushed together at the little school desks, perched on window sills or stood at the sides of the classroom. General Stewart introduced me with military precision and an economy both of words and enthusiasm : " This is Mr. Bannerman, the Liberal candidate, who wishes to address you ". I was greeted with banging of desks and clapping hands. I spoke for nearly an hour and then answered questions for at least another half-hour. The islanders were having a night out and there were demands for a ceilidh, but the chairman frowned on these suggestions and stood up to declare the meeting closed. Then he made a statement which took such breath as I had left away from me. He said in the dictatorial tones of the landlord to his tenants (for the majority of those present looked to him as their laird) : " After hearing Mr. Bannerman it is obvious that Liberalism has nothing to offer us, so I advise you all to vote Conservative. We thank Mr. Bannerman of course for coming to our island to address us ".

More accurately he should have said " my " island. Courteous to the death I have always found the Tory leaders, but none to pronounce the death sentence quite so blatantly and confidently as the general. He exercised his divine right so pleasantly that it was difficult for me to counter him (and he had kindly asked me to his house for a drink).

He was beginning to move off through the crush when I stopped him and halted the break-up of the meeting. I addressed the astounded islanders, many of whom were seated so close they could have touched us. I did not wish to harm them by asking them to pledge themselves publicly there and then to vote for me, for I knew the power of the laird over his subjects. Also, the general was an old man and within the limits of his military mind was congratulating himself on having routed the enemy with the minimum of discomfort.

" *A chairdean,* friends ", I said, " remember the ballot is secret and not even the general can find out how you vote. Let the convictions you hold as free men and women dictate how you vote. I am confident it will not be as the general commanded you ".

To the credit of the Coll islanders they erupted into enthusiastic cheers (led by the minister), banging their desk lids.

When I look back on it I should be grateful to the general for having done more in one sentence to bring me Liberal votes than I had done in my hour-and-a-half of talking. I am proud to know I had solid support of crofter and countryman still clinging to the land of his birth. As the old crofter in Tiree said to me one sunlit, breezy day on that beautiful isle of white sand and golden rye, as we sat " back of the dyke " discoursing on Highland injustice : " It's like this ", he told me in Gaelic, holding out a clenched fist, " *Sin agad Conservatism,* here you have Conservatism, *ach so agad Liberalism,* but here you have Liberalism " — and the fingers of his hand were spread wide.

Question time at my meetings out in the islands would be dull until I invited my audience to put their questions to me in Gaelic. From being mute when English was the medium they would become splendidly animated when using their native language. Then I got questions *gu leoir,* galore, and long discourses that taught me as much and more than I was able to impart. There is a moral here for anyone essaying to represent a constituency in the Highlands, or for that matter anywhere in Scotland. He can get closer to his people and represent them better if he speaks their language, whether it is Gaelic or Scots or even English with a Scots accent. An Oxford accent is no master key to parliamentary representation of the Scottish people.

I found the pier at Arinagour typical of the Government's neglect and apathy in Highland affairs. For lack of a little reconstruction it could not be used by any of the MacBrayne steamers and was served only by the occasional small cargo boat. The pier was built in the year of grace 1966, nearly ninety years after the islanders had first petitioned for the work to be done. The 22 farms in Coll had adjusted their economy to the lack of efficient transport, producing the famous little round Coll cheeses. Mainland competition and the setting up of the Milk Marketing Board (which did not cover the island) made even this export unprofitable. The only way therefore in which the agricultural exports of Coll could reach market was by rowing boat out to a steamer lying hove to at the mouth of the bay.

In July 1945 I was on board a MacBrayne steamer lying hove to, waiting for the small boat to come out. There was a stiff breeze blowing and the steamer heaved in the swell. As the boat hugged the shore on its way towards us we could distinguish two men tugging at the big sweeps, making slow and arduous passage to where the steamer lay. Standing precariously amidships in the little boat was a brown speckled cow tied by ropes to horns, head and — it seemed — every part of its body. At last when the boat was wallowing below us in the swell a gantry was swung out from the steamer and a belly band was lowered to it. This was fixed under the belly of the cow after a superhuman effort by the sailors while the boat was banging about against the steamer's side, and she was swung aloft. The tourists aboard — and there were many — were intrigued by this curious form of transport and rushed to focus their cameras on the hapless beast now sailing high above them. " The cow jumped over the moon ", remarked one of them, laughing. What with the rolling of the steamer, the swinging of the cow to and fro, and the shouting of the sailors, nothing so excitingly exotic and " native " had been witnessed by the tourists, unless they had seen something similar in the South Sea islands.

Then, I am glad to say, the frightened cow protested in the only way a good cross-Highland cow in that position could. It was fine to see the tourists scatter, though a bit unfair to make them suffer for the shortcomings of Highland transport. I wish that the Secretary of State for Scotland and all his entourage on their annual summer holiday survey of the Isles could have been underneath. That cow's protest against the primitive condition of Highland transport was assuredly more telling than the lukewarm speeches of those who then represented the Highlands in Parliament.

The day following my meeting on Coll, as if to emphasise the transport blockade which made living in the Highlands so difficult, Ray and I found that it would be three days before we could get off the island by MacBraynes. I therefore chartered a longboat from Mr. MacKenzie of the Crinan Hotel and, steered adroitly by himself, made the passage over to the island of Mull where we landed at the lovely and deserted bay of Calgary. It was from there, more than a century ago, that so many of Mull's finest families sailed in emigrant ships to Canada.

In Mull I found further object lessons on the disincentive to commercial endeavour in these remote areas. One crofter had been prevented from re-roofing his byre with corrugated iron because of the cost of transport from Glasgow. " It could be corrugated gold after I paid the transport ", was his comment. Another enterprising crofter told me how he had decided to expand his pig-keeping. He kept two pigs and fattened them on the food scraps from his house. When he bought a litter of nine pigs the food scraps were not sufficient to feed them and he brought in pig meal from a store in Greenock. He fattened his nine pigs — but when he counted the cost, inflated by transport charges, he found his profit was less than on the two pigs fed on scraps. Sadly he went back to keeping two pigs. Such examples are legion throughout the Highlands. Self-help dies because Westminster government neglects even the basic services and communications which are the minimal rights of citizens living within the United Kingdom.

When I campaigned so earnestly and optimistically in Argyll I reckoned without the vested interests of a Parliament in London, joined by 400 miles of bureaucratic red tape to St. Andrews House, Edinburgh, and thence by hundreds of miles of redder tape to the local councils throughout Scotland. I found that distance intensified the selfishness and indifference of those at the centre of power, both on the Left and Right. I reckoned also without the dynastic, *herrenvolk* opposition of the landowning class, who would be damned if they would allow even a moiety of their privileges to be taken from them, no matter how great the need or the plight of their fellow beings. The Conservative political faith fitted their selfishness like a glove. Those whose regard for the Highlands lies in the sport and privacy it can yield have imposed a stranglehold on the people who live there. There is some emancipation in the towns, but many people scattered through the great hinterland of mountain and glen are still under duress from the landlord, often an absentee. Security of tenure alone is not sufficient to counter the displeasure of the landlord. My own experience shows that where the landlord lives close by in his castle it is useless to hold a political meeting other than, of course, a Conservative one. Some crofters would not wish it to be known that they attended a political meeting which did not have the approval of the laird.

And so although injustice and neglect had been their lot for generations and progress has been stifled, most of the people still voted for the Conservative in Argyll. At the count I came a poor third to Conservative and Labour. For the first and last time I lost my deposit. It was a salutary lesson. I began to see clearly the powerful profile of the god called Establishment.

Because of victory, Tory governments felt it quite safe, for example, to forget about the pier at Carradale in Kintyre, for

which I had campaigned, which should have been built in the
'thirties to accommodate the forty fishing boats of the Carradale
fishermen and was not built until 1960 when only eight fishing
crews were left in the village. The revolution which I was prepared
to start at Westminster for comprehensive redress of the complex
Highland problems never got off the ground. I was a revolutionary
with no troops and few overt supporters. The yoke was on the
necks of the people, and when their masters were looking they
managed a strained smile; otherwise, in undertones, they complained
bitterly of their lot.

A "BONNIE FECHTER" IN
A DIRTY GAME

FEUDALISM and its twin Conservatism put paid to my Liberal hopes in Argyll in 1945, and off I hied by invitation to the county of Inverness in 1948. Inverness, I felt, might be more responsive than Argyll to Liberal views, and blood ties were closer as my mother was a Skye woman and my father a native of South Uist. Furthermore, I spoke Gaelic, and the county of Inverness was as yet more Gaelic than Argyll. But I reckoned without the town of Inverness. I made friends I shall always value in Inverness, but in general the kilt there had somehow become a symbol of class, and some incomers and non-Gaelic natives of the town operate an undercover apartheid that keeps the Gaelic native at arm's length. My Gaelic, an asset in the hinterland and in the islands, was, if anything, a drawback in the town.

Argyll is a big constituency but Inverness is bigger, stretching from the southern central Highlands to Beauly in the north-east and Mallaig in the west. Like Argyll it has its islands : Skye, Eigg, Muck, Rhum and Canna. Inverness, the county town, is the acknowledged capital of the Highlands. But political feudalism permeates society just as in Argyll. Even the larger towns, dependant as they are on tourism, are sometimes more reactionary than the country areas. My Liberal vote came in the main from the people of the hinterland, while the Tories had their main support in the larger towns, with the exception of such places as Kinlochleven and Fort William, where Labour was organised. The chief Conservative vote was to be found among the 10,000 electors of Inverness burgh.

Initially I posed no threat to the Establishment and was patronised by the hierarchy as a " bonnie fechter ". I even received some pre-election support in 1950 from Lord Lovat, the wartime Commando leader, but this was withdrawn after pressure was brought to bear on him. Even the fearless Commando cannot fight the Establishment. They explained to me that it would cause a " national crisis " if Lord Lovat, sitting on Conservative benches in the House of Lords, whose brother, Hugh Fraser, M.P., was prominent in Tory Parliamentary circles, offered to support a Liberal in Inverness-shire. It was my first indication of powerful forces moving behind the scenes.

My Tory opponent in the 1950 General Election was Lord Malcolm Douglas-Hamilton, who was genuinely concerned to improve the lot of the Highlands. He was the founder of the Highland Fund which, through its loans to the small man, was of inestimable value to the crofter and fisherman. The Douglas-Hamilton family are of Montrose quality. I knew well the late Lord David, youngest brother of the present duke, who was a keen student of Gaelic song and an able piper. His premature death when the plane he was piloting crashed on landing was a sore loss to this generation of Scotsmen.

Lord Malcolm Douglas-Hamilton won that election with a total of 16,000 votes. Although I came third behind the Labour candidate, it was some satisfaction to gather 8,000 votes, half as many as the Tory and, incidentally, more than John MacCormick had won in his three previous attempts — twice as a Scottish Nationalist and finally as a Liberal. What might time, patience and energy bring? I was more than determined to continue the fight, although I was coming to realise that politics was not just a matter of stating policies but an activity arousing animosity and many of the worst qualities in human kind.

I licked my wounds during the 1951 General Election and did not fight, but set to thereafter to try to dispel the apathy and resigned acceptance of injury and neglect which seemed to have become characteristic of Highland people. Lord Malcolm Douglas-Hamilton resigned in 1954 and in the by-election that year I reduced the Conservative majority from more than 10,000 to 1,300 in a three-cornered fight. Labour was relegated to a poor third. In the 1955 General Election I further reduced the Tory majority to 966. But I had just failed to make it. Even then I did not realise that I lacked the killer instinct, the cold expediency and instinct for intrigue necessary to counter the tactics of the Conservative leadership in Inverness county. It is ironic that in the end I was beaten by the impersonal, fanatical way in which the Tories collected the postal votes. I was told I polled more votes than the Tory on election day 1955, and would have won but for the postal vote.*

* Valid postal votes: 1,079. Bannerman's contention is, therefore, theoretically possible.

It was only when canvassing a house in a small township near Inverness that I appreciated fully the win-on-any-count organisation I was up against. Two old ladies lived there; the daughter, aged nearly 70, and her mother, whose age was 96. Apparently a lady of the manor had been in the habit of visiting them. The daughter, who knew me, made me welcome. When I asked about her vote she said it could not be anything but Liberal, but that "the lady" was getting a postal vote for her mother and she was afraid it would be Tory.

The mother was set deep in an armchair by the kitchen fire, bundled up in shawls and blankets, her little old face peeping forth like the face of a sleeping gnome. She looked as though she never moved from her chair and that it was bed for her as well. She was hardly of this world and her eyes were closed, though her daughter told me she was not asleep. I went over and spoke to her in Gaelic, asking her how she was keeping. Her eyes opened a little at the sound of my voice but she did not answer; instead, she started to recite a Gaelic psalm in quavering tones. She was far away from the world of politics, or indeed from any worldly interest. Her comfort was in her faith and the promise of the Psalms, certainly not in party politics. Unwilling to disturb her further, I bade her farewell. She murmured her *beannachdan,* blessings, and feebly patted my hand. I made my way from the house. The Tories could have her vote.

I shall also remember always with some shame for my race that there was one pocket of native Gaelic speakers in Glendale, Isle of Skye, who are said to have voted Tory by some devious conviction of their own, encouraged or directed by their minister. Of all the communities in the Highlands, this one, because of its radical Land League history, might have been expected to be Liberal. It is a sorry reflection that the very change in circumstances which transformed the folk of Glendale from being dependent crofters to owner-occupiers may have influenced them to forget the valiant fight their ancestors made for their present freedom and independence. It may be God's will that today they are Tories, but had their ancestors accepted that "God's will" which was synonymous with the will of the Establishment they would not now be the owners of their land.

The 1955 result was a narrow escape for the Tories, and from then until the 1959 General Election I continued to nurse the constituency. I was convinced that if I continued to fight in the county of Inverness, with the help of my many loyal friends and supporters I could eventually win. In the meantime, in 1957, I stood for the rectorship of Aberdeen University, and it was there I first realised fully to what lengths my opponents would go to baulk my political ambitions. Lord Hailsham, who had not then blotted his copybook by ringing bells and was the white hope of the Tories, appeared late on the scene as a contestant. He was Lord President of the Council at the time, and I began to suspect that war was being waged at some distance from Inverness. It surprised myself and shocked the Tory world when I beat Hailsham and became Rector.

Until then I had thought I had no enemies except political ones, but I had ignored the jealousies and selfish motives which even people one accounts as friends may have. I was also unaware of the methods which would finally be called into use against me by opponents with their backs to the wall. One method is called character annihilation, and the courteous gentleman is a master craftsman at spreading the poison. Always, of course, from a chalice of exquisite pattern. Having been saved by a few hundred votes, the Tory hierarchy of Inverness recognised in me a threat to their age-long privileges. Labour they could deal with, for Labour's threat was afar off. But mine was immediate. They laid their plans carefully and proceeded to use the whispering denigration with which they had routed MacCormick — some of it quite impossible to refute from the platform, for that matter even in private.

It is difficult to avoid bitterness, not only on my own account but because, with the parliamentary retention by the Tories at that time of the counties of Inverness, Ross and Cromarty, Caithness and Sutherland, and Argyll, the Highlands, crying out for social and economic redress, received none. Naturally the Tory Government in Westminster assumed that the people of the Highlands who licked the hand that spurned them, could be still further discounted.

The Crofters Commission was still deprived of the comprehensive powers that would enable it to reconstitute the crofting industry. The Taylor Commission had recommended far-reaching powers of road-making in townships and land settlement for the Crofters Commission. But the Tories would have none of it. Their cherished privileges in land and sporting estates would have been jeopardised and, besides, they said there was no money. There was no attempt to win approval for their party by paying attention to the manifest ills of a people suffering from even basic transport needs. No lifelines to the townships and to markets were constructed — which a people, if they were to continue to live in the modern world, desperately needed. On the contrary, freightage charges went up, piers were shut down and a major threat to the railways was made. Depopulation and unemployment increased disastrously. The Tory leaders with their imagined hereditary right to rule considered that they could go their own selfish way and fiddle while the Highlands burned, provided they held Highland fetes and marched in kilted splendour with outsize shepherd's crooks to the Highland Games. It was not until the 1964 General Election approached that anything of significance was done by the Government, which then acted with last-minute desperation.

I imagined that the apathy and neglect which the Tories continued to show in the face of the clamant needs of the area must eventually goad the majority of people to vote Liberal. But resignation, sycophancy and the fear of reprisal ingrown for generations are difficult to eradicate in a year or two. I made the mistake of assuming that it was just a political fight I had undertaken. On the contrary, what the Tory hierarchy was fighting for was its right of possession and authority.

For generations there has been no area of Great Britain where money could be more easily translated into real power over human beings than the Highlands. Whatever the origins of the money-making, as soon as it was exchanged for ownership of landed estates it bought not only modern comfort and privacy but dictatorial control over the lives of ordinary people. And if the landed estate was also associated with the corridors of party political power, then to challenge it was to be a Don Quixote tilting at the windmill.

Another factor in my final defeat in the 1959 election was the introduction of a Labour candidate, a young Fleet Street journalist who had been given the task of debunking me. He was a tub-thumping speaker whose declared aim was to attack " Bannermanism ". This election was his only appearance in the constituency. I thought it best to take little notice of him and so deprive him of more publicity than he could gather for himself. I have since realised that this was the greatest error of judgment in my political life, made against the advice of a loyal friend acting as my unpaid organiser, Bill McKell. I even shook the right hand this man offered me during the election when we met in an Inverness street, when in fact my right boot should have been my greeting.

At the same time the whispering campaigns intensified. They took the form of such malicious asides as : " Bannerman was carried drunk to bed in a Fort William hotel for five nights running. The hotel porter told me and he should know ". Then came truly vicious ones about Ray and my married life. If there is one success in my life it is the happiness of Ray and my family. But the rumours spread and some were bound to catch on — which was the aim of the Tory propagandists : Ray was leaving me, it was said. I found people, even those I accounted friends, looking askance at me. It was useless to try to refute scurrilous dirt from the patform, or indeed anywhere. They were forms of the old question which cannot be answered — had I stopped beating my wife? Only these were much more squalid. I was also supposed to be anti-Catholic in the Catholic areas and anti-Protestant in the Protestant districts.

From 1950 to 1959 is a long time for piling up dirt. False or not, dirt tends to stick, and, what is worse, spreads. Ultimately some self-important people who claimed to know me as a friend when I was likely to be successful, fed their resentment by retailing the smears when I failed.

I discovered that to be a fighter in politics one must be thick skinned and I am not. Success allows one to overcome much, but defeat is a breeding ground for lies and enmity. Familiarity also breeds contempt. I don't know that it reached that stage, but certainly my familiarity and my defeat were not a good combination. But while one side of the picture is dark, there is a shining contrast in the unselfish hard work and devotion and loyalty of thousands of kindly, generous people — to the cause and to myself. They live in my memory, making me proud and happy even though I failed to get the necessary number of votes up on the board.

In any case, I probably overstated my welcome. To nurse a constituency unsuccessfully for 11 years is too much of a strain on human kind, no matter how friendly and forbearing. So with the swing to Toryism which was general throughout the country in 1959 and the loss of votes which had previously been mine to the young Socialist, I lost the election by 4,000 votes. As a prophet in my own country I had run true to form.

It is not the ordinary Tory with whom I quarrel, but the arrogance of some of the leaders in political life and those who ape them socially. Their's is the same arrogance which has nearly destroyed the Highland people over the generations; the arrogance that could in the past burn and kill to make the land available for selfish use, the arrogance that so often worked maliciously in the background while the subservient factors did the dirty work.

I saw it at work in the case of a small shopkeeper (I shall call him Donald, though that is not his real name) who associated himself with the Liberal effort in his village in one of the islands. This qualified him for a visit from the local Tory leader — another military gentleman — who said courteously, and even with a joke : " Now then, Donald, this won't do your business any good ". Donald laughed, but as soon as his visitor had left with a cheerful, " Good morning, Donald, remember now ", he sat down and penned his resignation from his insignificant post in the local Liberal Association. Donald may still vote Liberal, but he no longer speaks or works for Liberalism. More important, he has ceased to think, act or speak as an independent, free man should.

Who has the right to blame the Donalds of the Highlands for not fighting back? They may have a shop, an hotel, a bit of land, a house — something for which they are beholden. They have their security and their family to safeguard and their living to make. They must be very independent not only in spirit but financially before they can openly offend the patronage of the Tory leaders who have immense social and economic influence in the community.

In politics I have encountered much intrigue, jealousy, some dishonesty, considerable misrepresentation and, when all else fails, character annihilation. (I believe I was accounted quite a decent chap before I entered politics.) My judgments on the political game do not stem from the chagrin of defeat. Although I would not minimise my personal disappointment, there is greater sadness in seeing friends and fellow workers who have striven so hard and so long rewarded by defeat.

Since anti-Establishment politics can escalate into a dirty game, why did I continue to play it? you may ask. Strangely enough, the fouls of the game are what make it more difficult to give up. Had I been unsuccessful in a clean game I would have moved out, beaten on policy or by my own deficiencies. But no one should run from the foul, nor should one trade fouls. Having been beaten in Inverness-shire by the combination of Tory and Labour and by the nationwide swing, I might have remained in the Highlands and waited for the tide to turn. But as chairman of the Scottish Liberal Party I felt we should fight the by-election of 1961 in Paisley. Even then I had no intention of fighting there myself. A forthright young industrialist called Vaughan Shaw had fought in Paisley twice before and was willing to have another go, but at the last moment had to withdraw. Rather than let the by-election go by default I decided to step in. I was influenced by the belief that wherever possible Liberals should take the opportunity of fighting industrial seats held by Labour. I still think we should adhere to this principle as widely as possible.

The result of the by-election was better than our highest hopes had led us to believe. I reduced a Labour majority of more than 7,000 to 1,600 and the Tory vote dropped from 21,000 to 5,600. I polled 17,542 votes. To put a Tory candidate, even such a pleasant one as G. R. Rickman, in danger of losing his deposit was a satisfactory and unusual occurrence for me. The result drew a typically condescending comment from the Prime Minister, Mr. Macmillan, at a Tory rally in Ayr two days later. He admitted disappointment with the result and went on, " but . . . I am not persuaded that the advent of a single Liberal swallow, even one crowned in the plumage of umpteen International caps, heralds the arrival of a neo-Asquithian summer ".

After such a result it would have been wrong for me not to remain in Paisley, and so I said goodbye to my direct endeavours to bring some legislative benefit to the Highlands. Win or lose in Paisley, I was most reluctant to take this decision, for it was my resentment against the depressed conditions prevailing in the Highlands and my fervent determination to win a new deal there which first brought me into active politics. However, I argued that to fight anywhere in Scotland was to fight against the suborning influence of central government.

The royal burgh of Paisley is one of the largest in Scotland, with nearly 100,000 inhabitants. Even with the burgh's fine record of house building, many of the older houses still occupied in Paisley lacked anything but the most primitive sanitation. The woman of nearly sixty to whom I spoke during the election campaign in her neat tenement flat said pathetically, " I've never lived in a house that had indoor sanitation ".

This was the kind of problem which concerned me most in Paisley, but once again I was unsuccessful in my attempt to reach the House of Commons. When eventually I entered Parliament, it was in another place.

15

AT THE HELM

" We adored John ", declares a leading Scottish Liberal. Even people who disagreed strongly with his views could be affected by the warmth of his personality, and it should be said that although Bannerman writes bitterly about the tactics employed against him in his Inverness-shire campaigns, he was never ungenerous to his opponents in the field. Perhaps he read more into the growing anti-Bannerman crusade than was justified. The young Labour candidate who came north from Fleet Street to challenge him in 1959 made it clear that he was fighting Bannerman rather than the Tory defender of the seat. His attack on Conservatism paled beside his onslaught on what he christened " Bannermanism ". His declaration that " I have come to kill Bannermanism stone cold dead in the glen ", is still remembered, and his robust tactics harmed the Bannerman cause without improving his own chances of election.

In 1955 Bannerman became chairman of the Scottish Liberal Party, a position he held for the next ten years, the years of Liberal revival in Scotland. In 1955 Jo Grimond was the lone representative in Westminster, but Bannerman's term of office ended in a blaze of glory as David Steel won a Border by-election and brought the number of Scottish Liberal M.P.s up to five. Only five Liberals contested Scottish seats in the 1955 general election; the number had risen to 26 in 1964. While Grimond emerged as a major force in British politics, it was always accepted during that time that Bannerman's was the voice of Liberalism in Scotland.

Such matters as the improvement and smooth running of the party machine he left to George Mackie, his right hand man and organising genius. Bannerman's gift was the ability to inspire enthusiasm. As chairman he might infuriate others by his cavalier disregard for formal procedure, which he was quite happy to ignore on occasion — and this sometimes helped him to steer a meeting clear of difficulties. At the height of an acrimonious and noisy executive meeting in a Bridge of Allan hotel he announced an unscheduled ten-minute tea break after which the debate continued in calmer fashion.

His prestige was immense. His determination to over-rule a minuted decision not to fight the Paisley by-election has already been mentioned. In any other situation an executive who flouted a democratic decision would have been sacked. Not Johnny Bannerman — from far and wide, supporters rallied loyally and enthusiastically to support him at the hustings.

During the later years of his chairmanship the spirit of nationalism was stirring, though it was not until he relinquished the post and became President of the Scottish Liberal Party that the Scottish National Party made its dramatic impact at the poll. This had a traumatic effect on Scottish Liberals who had regarded the nationalists in the early days as slightly errant Liberals who tended to extremism on the home rule issue. Since home rule was close to Bannerman's heart, he continually pressed for a working agreement with the S.N.P., in the face of determined opposition from George Mackie and Russell Johnston. The real S.N.P. threat to Liberal hopes became apparent when William Wolfe, the S.N.P. chairman, polled nearly 10,000 votes in virgin territory in industrial West Lothian and the Liberal lost his deposit. Thereafter Bannerman began to press for an understanding that Liberals and Scottish Nationalists would not compete in constituencies where one or other was strong. He argued that there should be truce between the two unless the nationalists put up candidates in seats held or threatened by Liberals. As the 1964 election approached, for example, it was decided — though the decision was not made public — not to back a Liberal in Perth and West Perthshire where Dr. Robert McIntyre had carried the S.N.P. flag for several elections in a row. He was regarded as a " Liberal " nationalist; therefore he should be given a free run.

The matter came to a head at two by-elections : Glasgow Pollok in March 1967 and Hamilton in November of the same year. At Pollok the nationalist George Leslie came a good third to Tory and Labour with more than 10,000 votes and the Liberal tail-ender polled a humiliating 734. At Hamilton the blonde lawyer Winifred Ewing scored the opportunist victory of the century by wresting a stronghold from Labour to become the first Scottish Nationalist M.P. since Dr. McIntyre's brief wartime tenure at Motherwell.

Not long after the Pollok by-election the Scottish Liberal Party conference was due to open in Perth. Polling day was March 9, and within days of the result Ludovic Kennedy, the writer and broadcaster who had recently returned to the land of his birth, announced that he would seek conference support for a pact with the nationalists. The motion was accepted for discussion by a narrow majority of the party executive, but in the event Arthur Donaldson, the S.N.P. leader rejected tentative Liberal advances in the brusquest terms.

Nationalists on the crest of the wave were unwilling to compromise. Hamilton came, Winnie Ewing forecast sweeping gains at the next general election and many Liberals had the uncomfortable feeling she might be right.

Different personalities at the top might have brought the two sides closer together, but when representatives met in a last-ditch attempt to bridge the gap both sides were intransigent. Bannerman (who had battled to substitute the word "opponent" for "enemies" in a resolution on Liberal-S.N.P. relations) sought in vain to attend the talks, where his sympathetic approach might have achieved something. The electoral pact was a dead letter.

16

HOME RULE

I⊤ is my dear wish to "make my people count", and no policy is closer to my heart than home rule for Scotland in domestic affairs. I believe that the Scottish Liberal Party must be more enthusiastic than in the past in advocating home rule. Our candidates should be known officially not merely as Liberal candidates, but as *Scottish* Liberal candidates. I believe too that the Nationalists and ourselves should refuse to butcher each other on the hustings to make a Roman holiday for Tory and Socialist. We should put the choice between our respective home rule policies—the moderate Liberal policy or the separatist policy of the Nationalists—squarely back in the lap of the Scottish people. This could be done by a plebiscite financed equally by the Scottish Liberal and the Scottish National parties. If the people of Gibraltar could settle their future by referendum, why not the Scots? I am willing to accept the decision of the Scottish people. Are the Nationalists?

The people of Scotland must do more than just sign their names to a polite request asking for home rule, and then go their way careless of whether their plea be answered or not, for the controlling powers in London seek in a thousand ways to denigrate and denounce the Scottish voice. The shackles will continue to grip if Scots give the impression they do not care. There may come a day when even the effort of signing names to a home rule petition may be asking too much, and, like slaves, our people become fearful of attaining the freedom so long denied them.

The centralised parties do not merely oppose and misrepresent nationalism in Scotland, they take no pains to hide their contempt for it. From their towers of power they proclaim themselves alone worthy to rule. Any party outside Tory or Socialist is regarded as a poor relation — and if there were a tradesman's entrance to the House of Commons, would be told to use it.

The Nationalists' extreme policy of complete separation can divide and weaken Scotland's voice and allow Tory or Socialist to rule us while we feud among ourselves. As chairman of the Scottish Liberal Party I made a statement in March 1964 which I stand by :

" Liberals in Scotland, England and Wales have always supported the de-centralisation of executive control from Westminster to the regional areas of the United Kingdom. These areas are manifestly the national areas of England, Wales and Scotland. At the 1961 Liberal Conference in Edinburgh the delegates from the three countries supported self-government for Scotland. Nowhere is there a place in Liberal policy for any separatism of the extreme character advocated by the Scottish Nationalists. For that reason there is no possibility of a pact with the Nationalists unless they agree to travel the Liberal road of federal home rule for the United Kingdom. The Scottish Liberal Party, although autonomous, is part of the Great Britain Liberal movement and would not contemplate any unilateral action for Scottish self-government in any case unnecessary, in view of the support of all Liberals in the United Kingdom for Scottish self-government.

We deplore the division of Scottish effort to obtain executive control of our domestic affairs through the extremism of the Scottish Nationalist views; for example, to have Scotland own and control a navy, army and air force, is not practical politics in this nuclear age, even if it was desirable.

We would be happy for the Nationalists to travel with us on the moderate Liberal road of self-government in our domestic affairs. This is practical politics which can be realised through the Scottish, English and Welsh Liberal vote. We consider our self-government programme to be an important part of the Liberal programme as a whole, ranking in priority with defence, co-partnership and other major Liberal policies ".

It has been suggested that Scottish Nationalists refuse to travel the Liberal road until self-government in domestic affairs is secured through a Parliament in Edinburgh because they are opposed to the faith of Liberalism. While they vote Nationalist, many — it is said — remain suspended Tories or Socialists. Though they might attain a portion of their aim by voting Liberal, it would appear they prefer to jeopardise everything — their ideal and ours — rather than vote for a party which fights Tory and Labour policies on a broad front. Nationalists will indignantly deny that their ultimate allegiance is to the Tory or Socialist parties. But how else can one judge their behaviour in rejecting the only credible political force which is pledged to attain the major part of their aims for Scotland?

Recently the Nationalists gained more support than ever in their history. This may not have reflected an increased acceptance of their extreme policy, but merely that they have devised better means of raising funds, improving organisation and getting propaganda coverage. The economic squeeze helped too. But I submit that when the Scottish people are informed fully of their responsibilities, financial and otherwise, under total independence, and of the extreme difficulty of bringing this about constitutionally, they will return to strengthen the Liberal home rule vote.

Scotland, though a small country, is a complicated amalgam of peoples, topography, and climate. She has a maldistribution of population which no country with direct control over her own destiny would tolerate. Let Scotland, therefore, become a true working partner in the Union by having her own Parliament. Complete control over finance and domestic affairs, and a share with the rest of the U.K. in defence, Commonwealth and foreign affairs, as defined in Russell Johnston's Home Rule Bill should satisfy most Scots. Let the Nationalists consider it an interim policy if they wish, or a mile-stone on their road to complete independence. But if their attitude is all or nothing, the odds are great that Scotland will get nothing.

17

INTERLUDE: A GROUSE MOOR SAFARI

Question: What would your comment be on the suggestion that the Highlands be turned into a great game reserve?

John Bannerman: Unprintable!

—from *Point Blank*, a Grampian television programme broadcast in 1966.

LET the tycoons be assured of halcyon days on the " Glorious Twelfth ", with the purple heather moor stretching away to the distant blue hills and only the grouse to call " Go back, go back! " The people can go hang! As far as the eye can see — only wonderful space and privacy — though unfortunately here and there eyesores break the sweeping contours of the moor. On a closer look these are seen to be the ruins of croft houses, with the remains of their pathetic little byres attached. Nettles and ivy spread to cover their shame. The gnarled rowan tree bends over the broken-down wall.

Bang! Bang! go the guns. Go back, go back, cry the grouse on this beautiful heather waste . . .

Laughter and quiet humour make the alfresco lunch a gay affair. Cold grouse, oatcakes, brandy, whisky and coffee help. The old tweeds have lain often on the heather. It is an informal affair, but with unwritten rules which no shot worthy of the name would dream of violating. The ghillies (the " boys ") are lunching discreetly out of earshot, though not too far away. The shooters begin to stir. Sir Jocelyn shouts and the head keeper or head ghillie, who seems to have been expecting the summons, moves up to the party.

" There's some brandy and whisky, Donald — take it. And there are some cold grouse and sandwiches left over if you care to have them too ", says Sir Jocelyn.

Donald thanks him quietly and takes the leavings back to share with the "boys" — *fuighleach,* scraps, from the purple heather table which for that lunchtime at least is the table of the rich.

The sun is strong, all is well with the world — the wide, handsome world of the shooters. An afternoon's sport lies ahead. A final drink at the tumbling mountain stream; the dogs jump and whimper, the shooters adjust their cartridge belts, load their guns, space out across the hill with the ghillies and dogs between them, and it's away over the endless purple of the moor. On safari! Where else would such peace, power and privacy be obtained?

In past years Sir Jocelyn has stridden over the deserts and through the jungles of Africa and India, brave and unconcerned, with his boys in single file behind him ready to spread out and beat up the ground not for deer but for tigers or elephants to be shot by Sir Jocelyn's gun. But in those countries, unlike the Highlands, Sir Jocelyn had done something to justify his rights. Now he has been sent packing by the developing people of the world. Ready and waiting are the beautiful empty spaces of the Highlands of Scotland, part of the great island known abroad as England.

For two centuries they have been neglected : the people evicted from their homes and crofts, the land turned over to sheep and to deer forests and grouse moors.

Not all the Sir Jocelyns are strangers from the southland. Some bear the proud clan names of chiefs who once spoke the language of their people. But long since they have been measured by the London yardstick. Where they counted their clan family, they now count sheep and deer, grouse and salmon. They have their pieces of silver. The children of the heather are scattered *mar mholl air la gaoithe,* like thistledown on a windy day.

The Clearances of the Highland people started a long time ago, but the *laraich* or crumbling foundations of croft and shieling can still be seen today throughout the Highlands. They are now covered with nettles whose sting is slight compared to the sting of memory recalling the cruel persecution of those far-off days. Naked greed actuated the Establishment of the day — government, landlords and factors — to burn homes and harry great communities of people throughout the Highlands on to the rocks of the shore and to far corners of the earth — a people whose simple way of life made them vulnerable, a people whose sons were dying " for king and country " on the battlefields of Europe.

It is said that during the early years of the reign of Queen Victoria the Isle of Skye alone gave to the army 666 officers, ten thousand other ranks and 120 pipers. There is hardly that number of people in Skye today.

Then as now the Highlander has been a hero in war, but merely a " ghillie " in peace. As the Gaelic poet has it : " When help was needed in the Great War, grouse or snipe on the face of the hill were no use, nor deer of the thin horn, nor yet the hornless sheep. Face the enemy with these and see if they can wield the strong arm. Had the fine boys in France had the freedom of the gun and steed and the hunting of their own moors, these days would not be so dire nor victory so hard. Nor would the soil of France enfold so many of our sons ". The pleas of the poets have echoed down the centuries in the hearts of Highlanders. Is the debt repaid by making a human wilderness where sport and sheep are supreme and the taking of a salmon and a bit of venison for the house a criminal offence? Legislative help could have made the Highlands a country of happy, contented families like Norway.

The Highlander has served Britain honourably and bravely on the battlefield, but London government's only answer to succeeding generations has been : Get out! Emigrate!

The Isle of Mull, in common with many parts of the Highlands, continues to lose its youngest and most enterprising men and women. To take their place come the retired from all walks of life, looking for privacy and peace. Many have bought estates for the price of a town bungalow and oppose the development of the island — for development would mean people, and that would be inconvenient and disturb privacy.

Returning one autumn day by the MacBrayne steamer from Tobermory to Oban, I talked with a photographer from Newcastle. It had been his first visit to Mull and he was enthusiastic about its wonderful kaleidoscope of colours — the russets, the yellows, the browns, the greens, the deep blue of the distant mountains, the sparkle of its limpid sea coves and clean white stretches of sand. But he was returning to Newcastle bewildered and resentful.

He had parked his car on a narrow road by the seashore with not a habitation in sight. A tweedy gent, as he described him, appeared from nowhere and told him in no uncertain terms to move on; not, my Newcastle friend insisted, because the road was private, but because there was " no parking allowed in these parts ". The beauties of Mull were dimmed for the Newcastle man. Tweedy gents want neither tourist nor crofter.

I visited a township in Skye in 1963 where good houses had been evacuated in the last ten years and only three remained occupied.

The township was situated in a sheltered glen of considerable fertility. The time was midnight and I went with the local doctor, called out on an emergency to one of the three occupied houses.

We drove as far as a side road reached; it simply petered out in the moorland. From there we journeyed slowly and perilously on foot by the aid of the doctor's flashlight, avoiding the worst of the bog holes. But it took us about twenty minutes of stumbling around in the darkness before we reached the house.

Over the previous thirty years a road could have been made by the authorities, even of the cart-track variety, to save the people and serve the township. But no money has ever been made available for this type of unclassified road construction.

The ordinary Highlander has never been able to appreciate why hundreds of millions of pounds could be wasted on ground nuts, or given in colonial subsidies, or lost on abortive nuclear weapons, when £25 million in the hands of a development board could transform the Highlands, half the area of Scotland, from a depopulated wilderness into a thriving growth area for folk and food.

The record is a long indictment of apathy and neglect, a tale of lost opportunities such as that presented by the 1938 Hilleary Report. This was a blueprint for comprehensive rehabilitation of the Highlands and islands, widely acknowledged to contain the essential remedies for social and economic rebirth. It was voted the " munificent " grant of £65,000 per annum by the government and even that was withheld because of the war. Of that sum £30,000 per annum was supposed over five years to build adequate roads and piers. Yet as the report indicated, 208 districts had no access road.

At that time nearly half a million pounds was being spent annually in the Highlands by the Government in dole and public relief. Even such a sum spent annually in a constructive planned manner would have given hope to this hopeless region of Great Britain. But the Tory Government wasted the taxpayers' money and at the same time undermined the morale of the Highlander by denying him a job and essential communications with the outside world.

" Oh that the peats would dig themselves and the fish jump from the sea ! " is the sarcastic representation of the Highlander's attitude because he refuses to join in the rat race against time. But the Highlander is not lazy. He is as willing as the next man to work if he sees profit in his work. But in the Highlands, time is about all the Highlander can enter on the assets side of his balance sheet. And perhaps there are profits more valuable than material when time is not the miserly master but the generous servant.

"Time southers a'", time heals everything. But time does not make wrong right. The annals of history disclose a continuing oppression and neglect of my race. The same disregard for human rights still obtains. As recently as 1948 seven crofters of Knoydart staked out a few acres extra from an estate of 100,000 acres in the hands of a financier lord, in order to make their crofts a little more economic. But the Socialist government of the day sided with the lord and six of the crofters eventually had to leave.

The Seven Men of Knoydart and their shameful treatment are added to the scroll of recorded injustices meted out to the Highlander for generations. As long as the great party political machines control us from London, so long will injustice continue towards the remote areas. As for the financier lord, he saw no reason, when nobody said him nay, why he should not deal with the land and his crofters as he would with his stock exchange shares.

18

NEW HOPE FOR THE HIGHLANDS

NOT until 1965 was the Highlands and Islands Development Board set up. It was made law by a Labour Government, but it was directly the result of long, continuing pressure by Liberals for a new deal for the Highlands, presented to the people over the last twenty-five years from election platforms. It should also be noted that it came into being only after representation of the Highlands in Parliament by the Tories had almost ceased to exist. Freedom for the Highlands under the Tories was freedom to rot.

The fight, however, is not yet won. Unfortunately in the history of the United Kingdom the excuse for not spending money on the Highlands has always been that Britain had little to spare, and that other purposes had prior claim. We seem to be in no different position in this year of grace. The Labour Government failed to fulfil many of its election commitments through having no money to finance them. If it is a question of place by priorities, then the Highlands, which have been queueing up for half-a-century for attention, should now be near the front. If any project has to be shelved or curtailed, it should not be the rehabilitation of the Highlands and its people. They have waited long.

Although Labour and Tory governments in the past had the democratic obligation to legislate for the whole country, they have neglected Scotland and totally forgotten the Highlands, with the result that today only four per cent of the population of Scotland lives in the Highland half of the country. No country, especially an industrialised country like ours, can afford such a maldistribution of population. It will not be easy to redress the balance : widespread land settlement, a new, progressive spirit in the indigenous industries of agriculture, forestry and fishing, the introduction of new industries — all encouraged by cheaper transport and better communications.

As long as I can remember, the high cost of freightage has made the Highlands the area of Britain with the highest cost of living. Relief should be given to reduce this burden for a period of at least twenty years so that new industry may not be discouraged from coming into the Highlands, and indigenous industry may be given profitable lifelines to the central markets. If this were done the Government's expenditure in reducing the freight charges would be recouped through increased revenue brought in by increased initiative and spontaneous development.

Bitter experience makes one fear that sufficient financial backing will not be made available for the comprehensive rehabilitation of the Highlands. But if the Highlands and Islands Development Board is to tackle land use in the Highlands effectively, the Treasury must be more generous than in the past.

Of the more than nine million acres of land in the seven crofting counties, there are a million acres under bracken, half-a-million requiring arterial drainage, and a million requiring settlement and rehabilitation of a general agricultural character. There remains several million acres of deer forests, including the mountains of the Highlands, which should be surveyed to determine the proportion which can carry sheep and hill cattle, how much should be afforested, how much left free to carry deer and grouse, how much of special attraction should be made accessible to tourists.

In developing the use of land, the board should not merely acknowledge crofting to be "a way of life", but must stimulate it as a business venture. Crofting has many blessings attached to it, but until recently cash income was not high on the list. Yet there is no reason why crofting should not increase its return by at least twenty-five per cent, using the original Stapledon methods of grass improvement and reclamation.

Land settlement on a comprehensive scale should be the first main project of the Board, so that a prosperous, numerous and contented people could be established on the land. The £1 million offered by the Labour Government for super-hotels in the Highlands could be better used in a Government programme for land settlement which would be of untold benefit. Hotels in any case will be built by the hotel industry as the country is opened up and develops. The Government has enough to do with its money; building schools, hospitals, clearing slums, settling the land, building roads — the list is endless. So often it gets its priorities blurred to the detriment of the Highlands.

It is often necessary to enlarge small-holdings or crofts to give an economic return, but a recent Government bribe to ageing small-holders to quit is but another bureaucratic stratagem which will rid the land of its people. It is a lazy (and cheaper!) method compared with trying to bring in small industries which might give part-time employment to small crofters, and it sidesteps the issue of the reclamation and resettlement of hundreds of thousands of sporting acres of land at present in private ownership. To clear people off the land by bribery is a cynical return to the era of the Clearances. There are many methods of husbandry by which small areas of arable land can be lived on, providing there are ancillary jobs available.

Why does the Board place so much importance on the establishment of an industrial conurbation around Invergordon? Welcome as the project may be, it is significant that the Board has failed to plan first of all to bring life and hope to the indigenous, basic industries of agriculture, forestry, fishing and the woollen and tourist industries. The basic economic fabric of the whole Highlands is tattered and torn and needs repair. As it is, the only spontaneous growth areas are the towns and burghs, to which the countryside already exports its people. Why add another magnet in the form of a new industrial conurbation, drawing population away from the country areas of the Highlands, before the task of restoring life to the countryside has been tackled?

A register of those wishing to return or to migrate to the Highlands was compiled by the Board. But does it presuppose the provision of land for wide-scale land settlement? Twenty years ago there was said to be upwards of four thousand applications for small-holdings in the files of St. Andrew's House, Edinburgh. Time may have disposed of many of the applicants. The Department of Agriculture may have classified the balance, but it has assuredly not satisfied it. No land settlement of any scale has been essayed since the 'twenties. Since 1945 less than 50 people have been settled by direct Government action on the nine million acres of the Highlands.

One essential is that light industries should be established in country areas so that farmers of land which does not yield a living wage should have the chance of augmenting their incomes at the local factory. I think the industrial crofter is worth planning for. But only after light industries are introduced all over the Highlands as a corollary to purposeful land use and settlement should the Board seek to develop conurbations of the Invergordon variety.

In any case, such urban growths would develop of their own accord if the social and economic fabric of the Highland countryside were successfully renewed. Renewal would require the establishment of co-operative marketing centres, arterial drainage schemes, and new roads. Today land reclamation moves at a snail's pace and only here and there in the Highlands. Liming and manuring and reseeding should be speeded up by the use of plane, helicopter and caterpillar vehicles. The limiting factor is finance, but dividends are never secured without investment. In this case there is a certain long-term return which the Government should underwrite.

As a Forestry Commissioner for over eleven years, I am aware of the rivalry that has existed between the forester and the farmer. This has never been resolved, and the hill sheep and upland farmer still views the activities of the Forestry Commission with suspicion. It should be one of the chief objects of the Board to bring the interests of farming and forestry in the Highlands closer together. This could be more easily done to the mutual advantage of farmer and forester if one authority instead of two or three as at present — further bedevilled by the influence of the private landlord — had control of land use. In other words, the Department of Agriculture and Fisheries should have Forestry added to it. This would have the further advantage of taking the control of forestry in Scotland away from the centralised authority in London* and vesting it directly with the Secretary of State, or preferably with a Scottish Minister for Agriculture, Forestry and Fisheries.

I favour, too, the proposal of the Lochaber Crofters' Association which would marry forestry and crofting so closely that the crofter could be helped to plant and own trees on his croft grazings and thereby acquire capital as the trees come to marketable use. An important development of land use in the Highlands would also be a further establishment of forest holdings. The record of the Forestry Commission shows that the holdings already formed add considerably to food production by encouraging the farming of cattle, sheep, pigs and poultry, and add to the income of the forestry workers. Enthusiasm for forest holdings has cooled in the last decade, but I feel that this form of land settlement should be persisted in, even though work on holdings may reduce optimum work in forestry.

Another important area of attention for the Board should be the encouragement of hydro-electric resources. Governments have held up development in this generation, influenced no doubt by the competing interests of oil, coal, gas and nuclear power. It

---

* Since Bannerman wrote these words the Forestry Commission has been on the move. The headquarters, at Basingstoke, are at last destined for Scotland.

should always be remembered that the far-seeing hydro-electric development of the Highlands was carried out without expense to the taxpayer. This made the standstill order, instituted by a Tory government and continued by Labour in spite of an unsatisfied demand for electricity in the U.K. as a whole, the more iniquitous. It is to be hoped that the Board will aim to set the turbines going again.

If there is one direction other than transport in which I would not object to nationalisation it is in the sphere of piped water supply. Undoubtedly if the amenities of ordinary living are to be available to a redeveloped Highlands there must be piped water for the houses in every township. Here again the Highlands and Islands Development Board could be the catalyst.

Lastly, I would advocate that any comprehensive rehabilitation of the Highlands must be founded on a favourable flat or tapering rate on imports and exports to and from the Highlands. On the west coast and the islands, for example, full use has not been made of piers even when they have been repaired or rebuilt, because freight charges were so prohibitive that they formed a blockade around the Highlands as effective as anything devised by submarine warfare.

This programme for the rehabilitation of the Highlands is no different from the Liberal programme preached up and down the *Gaidhealtachd,* Gaeldom, over the last forty years. In 1945, for example, I gave an address to the Royal Philosophical Society of Glasgow in which I proposed a basis for the reconstruction of the economy of the Highlands which today might well go under the heading of regionalism. To deal with a region effectively there must be a real devolution of executive authority and adequate finance. Unless a Government is prepared to give power freely away from the centre to duly elected representatives of the people at regional level, remoteness of control and increasing bureaucracy defeats the best laid schemes of the planners. It is the people who must count.

As for the Highland people, there is much they can do themselves. But the wholesale renewal of their economic fabric is beyond them. It has been the attitude of succeeding London governments to shrug off the blame for the present situation and to sneer, albeit circumspectly, at the remnant of people left. The Highlander has been condemned as lazy and always waiting for someone to help him. But the blame rests squarely on apathy and the neglect of the Highlands by governments over the generations. If there are sneers, they should be reserved for Westminster.

19

ANOTHER PLACE

THWARTED in his ambition to enter the House of Commons, Bannerman came at last to Westminster as a life peer. His first appearance on the red benches of the House of Lords caused a sensation for that calm and somnolent place. He was introduced in his robes just after 2 p.m. on Wednesday, December 6, 1967, and two hours later he was on his feet speaking — only the second peer on record to make his maiden speech on the day of his introduction. It was a fighting speech, delivered with a fire and passion strange in that House, and it created such a stir that he was immediately interviewed for a weekend Westminster television programme — during which he launched into Gaelic for good measure. The subject of debate was Scotland, and Bannerman declared roundly that " as soon as the equivalent House is set up in Edinburgh I shall gladly take the shorter journey ".

Bannerman took as his title Lord Bannerman of Kildonan in the County of Sutherland, Kildonan being the strath from which his ancestors were forced at the time of the Clearances. There had been hint of a peerage earlier during the Wilson administration. In spite of his feelings about aristocracy and privilege, Bannerman had no qualms about accepting a life peerage — it gave him another platform from which to shout for Scotland.

This he did with dogged persistence from the day of his maiden speech when he rumbustiously attacked the selective employment tax for its effect on the Highlands, high freight rates in the crofting counties, and suggested that Highland landlords should make over their sporting estates at a fair rent to tenants who would undertake to develop them for agriculture. His last speech in July 1968, on the Transport Bill, returned to the matter of subsidies for Highland transport and accused the Government of killing off the Edinburgh-

Hawick railway line. He protested about the closure of Highland schools, he attacked the Government-subsidised MacBrayne shipping line for by-passing Highland quays, he had a notable passage of arms with Lord Hughes, then Minister of State for Scotland, on the laws governing inheritance in the crofting counties, and when a report on winter sports in the Cairngorms was debated he deprecated that it wrote off the development of farming in the area : to him, the first priority was " folk and food ".

Even in the short time he attended the House of Lords he made his presence felt — from breaking a chair (by accident) in the peers' tea room to downright refusal to vote with his party for the renewal of sanctions against Rhodesia in 1967. The Conservative opposition under Lord Salisbury were trying to use their majority in the Lords to defeat the sanctions order and it was critical that Liberal peers should vote with the Government to prevent this happening. But Bannerman's loyalty to the Montrose family (the Duke of Montrose being prominent in the Smith cabinet) overrode his allegiance to the party line and he resisted all pressure from an enraged Lord Byers to bring him to heel. When he felt strongly on an issue, no one could shake him.

At the Liberal Assembly in Edinburgh in the autumn of 1968 he looked forward to his return to Westminster in the new year, but he was already a dying man.

20

LOOKING BACK

Looking back on life, there is no room for cheating by taking bits here and there and saying, " This was fair and that was braw ". Life's fabric is indivisible and must be taken as a whole.

Happiness has nothing to do with material success or failure, both of which I have experienced. My yardstick is the family. The family is the ideal unit for sharing grief or happiness — and with no desire to sentimentalise, I give my family as the corner stone of my life.

If there is benefit to be distilled from being born a Scot, it is because we realised " lang syne " that there is no unit in which the qualities of love and loyalty have a better chance of developing than in the family. Where the family spirit is strong and healthy, then the spirit of village, town and nation will be strong and healthy also. The family is Scotland's bulwark against the erosion of our standards as a nation. Change may be the law of nature and nation, but, as in nature, change should be a renewal.

My debt as an individual is therefore clearly entered first as a son of Highland parents whose precept and example left me with little choice but to try to repay them. Astray I went, and often, but I couldn't get far. Always the threads of love and example held me, stronger far than any chains of confinement or dictation. These are forged but to be broken, the other kind are unbreakable. I have had two families, and it is to the second even more than to my boyhood family that I owe lifelong happiness. In the first the balance was upset when my mother died when I was young and my father became the all-important influence. In the second, the influence of Ray has been supreme, not only over the children but over myself.

Ray is the only daughter of the late Walter Mundell of Dalchork, near Lairg in Sutherland. The Mundell name is one to conjure with in farming, not only in Sutherland and Ross but in south Argyll and Ayrshire as well. On a trip north to Lairg Provincial

Mod with my father — he adjudicating, I singing — I met
the brown-eyed daughter, a descendant of the Mundells from the
south of Scotland who brought the *caoraich mhaola,* the hornless
sheep, north to replace the people who had been evicted. (The
pendulum has swung full circle. The Strath of Kildonan from
which my ancestors were evicted is not so far from Lairg.)

As with my father, so with Ray. I speak of her not because I wish
to impress on the reader my own infinite debt to her, but because
she is directly responsible along with so many mothers for the
Scotland I love, and hope to see rising from its knees while there
is yet time to become an inspiring and active partner in a resurgent
United Kingdom.

If " hame and infancy " conjure up for us Scotland, how evident
it should be to all that it is the mother that glorifies both images.
I therefore give you a toast : to Ray. You who drink with me will
see your own wives in the glass.

Although Ray and I have tried to work for Scotland in a number
of ways, our multiplication to four families and, at the time of
writing, ten grandchildren — the whole with a good, liberal Scots
upbringing — is our most successful contribution. May you, my
reader, find satisfaction of a similar character filling your heart
at the end of the day . . .